SERVING
THE CHURCH,
REACHING
THE WORLD

SERVING
THE CHURCH,
REACHING
THE WORLD

In honour of D.A. Carson

Edited by Richard M. Cunningham

ivp

INTER-VARSITY PRESS
36 Causton Street, London SW1P 4ST, England
Email: ivp@ivpbooks.com
Website: www.ivpbooks.com

First published 2017

British Library Cataloguing-in-Publication Data
A catalogue record for this book is available from the British Library

ISBN: 978-1-78359-593-8
eBook ISBN: 978-1-78359-594-5

Set in Monotype Garamond 11/13pt
Typeset in Great Britain by CRB Associates, Potterhanworth, Lincolnshire
Printed and bound in Great Britain by Ashford Colour Press Ltd, Gosport, Hampshire

Inter-Varsity Press publishes Christian books that are true to the Bible and that communicate the gospel, develop discipleship and strengthen the church for its mission in the world.

IVP originated within the Inter-Varsity Fellowship, now the Universities and Colleges Christian Fellowship, a student movement connecting Christian Unions in universities and colleges throughout Great Britain, and a member movement of the International Fellowship of Evangelical Students. Website: www.uccf.org.uk. That historic association is maintained, and all senior IVP staff and committee members subscribe to the UCCF Basis of Faith.

CONTENTS

Part III

LIST OF CONTRIBUTORS

Kirsten Birkett teaches Ethics, Philosophy and Church History at Oak Hill College. Kirsty has previously worked for the Universities of New South Wales and Sydney and taught at Moore Theological College. Her many publications cover the relationship between science and religion. She has also written on psychology, feminism and the family for both a popular and an academic audience.

Richard M. Cunningham is married to Ruth and they have five children. He is an ordained Anglican minister and member of the Church of England College of Evangelists. After working for churches in London and Oxford, he became Director of the Universities and Colleges Christian Fellowship (UCCF) in 2004.

William Edgar is married to Barbara and has two adult children. He is Professor of Apologetics at Westminster Theological Seminary, Philadelphia, where he has taught for twenty-nine years, and *Professeur Associé* at the Faculté Jean Calvin, Aix-en-Provence. Bill is a popular international speaker and author and an accomplished jazz pianist who directs the jazz band *Renewal*.

Stefan Gustavsson is married to Ingrid and has three adult children. He is the General Secretary of the Swedish Evangelical Alliance and the Director of the Centre for Christian Apologetics in Stockholm. Stefan has authored several books on Christian apologetics and the Christian mind, and writes regularly for different Swedish magazines.

David Jackman is the former president of The Proclamation Trust and founded the Cornhill Training Course. He was the Senior Minister of Above Bar Church, Southampton, for eleven years, prior to which he was Universities Secretary for UCCF. He is author of at least fourteen books and runs international preaching workshops for pastors. He and his wife, Heather, have two adult children.

Michael Keller is married to Sara and they have two young daughters. He has been a pastor of churches in Boston and New York for over twelve years and is a popular speaker at universities. He is currently enrolled in a PhD programme, while planting a new church in Manhattan called Redeemer Lincoln Square.

Tim Keller is married to Kathy and they have three sons. He is an ordained minister in the Presbyterian Church in America. Tim taught at Westminster Seminary for five years and for the past twenty-eight years has been pastor of Redeemer Presbyterian Church in New York City and an international church planter and best-selling author.

Michael J. Ovey, before his sudden and unexpected death on 7 January 2017, was the Principal of Oak Hill Theological College. Mike was an ordained Anglican minister and worked first as a curate under Andrew Cornes at All Saints, Crowborough, and then as a lecturer at Moore Theological College, Sydney. His PhD was in the field of trinitarian theology. He is survived by Heather and their three children.

J.I. Packer serves as the Board of Governors' Professor of Theology at Regent College in Vancouver, where he has taught since becoming Professor of Systematic and Historical Theology in 1979. After his conversion through the Christian Union at Oxford (OICCU) he became one of the most significant evangelical theologians of the twentieth century. *Knowing God* is one of his many publications. Jim is married with three children.

John Piper is founder and teacher of desiringGod.org and chancellor for Bethlehem College and Seminary. For thirty-three years he served as pastor of Bethlehem Baptist Church, Minneapolis, Minnesota. He is author of more than fifty books, including *Desiring God* and *Let the Nations be Glad!* John is married to Noël and they have five children and twelve grandchildren.

John Stevens is the National Director of the Fellowship of Independent Evangelical Churches (FIEC) and a founding pastor of City Evangelical Church Birmingham, and remains a leader of Christchurch Market Harborough, which he planted in 2011. Prior to full-time ministry he taught law at the University of Birmingham, where he served as Deputy Head of the Law Faculty. He and his wife, Ursula, have four children.

FOREWORD

Dick Lucas

What is it about this man D.A. Carson that stirs in me, as in so many, thoughts of affection and admiration? The book you hold in your hand will provide reasons aplenty why this is the case. Thank you, esteemed contributors, for what you have written so fully and so well, in honour of our teacher and friend.

But I must speak for myself. A word that comes immediately to mind is loyalty: Don remains unashamed of people and particulars that human nature finds it easy and convenient to leave behind.

First there is the Gospel of Christ, of which Dr Carson remains entirely unashamed. Surely it is a grand encouragement, if a rare sight, to see a distinguished academic sallying forth from his study to evangelize today's benighted students. Yet this very unusual Don, as I must take leave to describe him, is quick to take opportunities to defend and declare the truth, in order to gain allegiance to his Lord and Master. May God raise up many such able men to do likewise.

Then there are the holy Scriptures of which our friend is a most distinguished exegete and commentator. In my time, mid-twentieth century, newly commissioned pastor-teachers had all too little to help them, compared with today's riches in terms of Bible commentaries, both scholarly and true to apostolic standards. I like that sentence in the preface to the Pillar series that Don is providing for preachers and serious students: 'If the text is God's word, it is appropriate that we respond with reverence, a certain fear, a holy joy, a questing obedience.'

I find in my copy of Carson on John instructions for my executor, including the words 'a fine commentary: into whoever's hands it should fall, read it!' Alas, by that time this blue treasure may have fallen apart through constant use.

A favourite recollection of mine comes from the wonderful *Memoirs of an Ordinary Pastor*. We discover Don's father going through a book his son has written, and jotting down notes, ticks and question marks in the margin. Reading Carson Junior on penal substitution as making sense of all the other things that the Bible says about the death of Christ, Carson Senior scribbles alongside, 'No sign of liberalism here!' Men of my generation will most appreciate this, for this was the era when the older preachers were weary, not without good reason, of the wretched betrayals emanating from the corridors of the theological schools of their time.

For my third choice, I would cite commitment to the concerns of today's 'ordinary pastors'. Obviously Dr Carson will be in demand for the big assemblies, and to counsel the growing body of doctoral students, and the like. But what I see is an equal devotion to stand with less prominent groups, the men at work in isolated parts of the world, and the warriors battling unbelief in the tougher areas. This professor is no stranger to the struggle against the powers of this dark world, having long since renounced a peaceful ivory tower.

My old dictionary is not always able to get it quite right; but under 'loyalty' I find 'a strong feeling of support or allegiance'. I know that God has graciously implanted just such deep concerns to support others in the heart of our friend and teacher. And for that I am thankful.

London, UK

EDITOR'S INTRODUCTION

Richard M. Cunningham

Upon realizing that Don Carson would turn 70 shortly before coming to speak at the UCCF London-wide mission, I rather foolishly asked his permission to celebrate this milestone with a party. Don liked the idea so much he threatened to pull out of the entire trip.

Noting his aversion to personal attention and any whiff of celebrity culture, I decided – with regard to this Festschrift – that it would be far simpler to crave Don's forgiveness after publication than to seek his permission in advance. Aware of Don's likely ire, not to mention the hard work involved, I was gratified that such able and busy Christian leaders were willing to contribute essays with relatively little arm-twisting; such is the esteem and affection held for D.A. Carson on both sides of the Atlantic. 'Serving the Church, Reaching the World' suggested itself as the theme of this book for two reasons.

First, Professor Carson's entire ministry, from what I can see of his publishing and speaking commitments, seems to be shaped by this twin desire to serve the church and to reach the world. Secondly, back in 2007 when UCCF decided to start the New Word

Alive conference, I phoned Don at home to explain that having paid a deposit on the venue, we had neither speakers nor a programme, 'So could you please help us?' Sensing the significance of this event, Don not only cleared existing diary commitments to join us but also persuaded John Piper to do likewise, and in so doing helped us launch a significant annual Easter Conference that has as its mission statement 'Serving the Church, Reaching the World'.

As church influence in the West diminishes, the temptation for confessional evangelicals to move towards a pragmatic, open evangelicalism will grow. The chapters in this volume are intended to equip the serious-minded reader with those biblical convictions that will enable us to be more effective both in formal ministry and in ordinary witness to our increasingly secular society without compromising biblical priorities and truth. It is my hope that the convictions expressed in this volume will also encourage confessional evangelical leaders to be even more outward-looking and less inclined to fight phoney wars with each other.

Part I

The first two chapters focus on the primacy of preaching and the importance of doing it God's way. The Lord's primary means of reaching the world is through the local church and David Jackman's 'Preaching that Changes the Church' provides a succinct and practical overview of the importance of effective expository preaching. This is followed by Jim Packer's 'Preacher and Theologian: The Ideal Christian Communicator', which demonstrates the importance of systematic theology (in particular) to the preacher.

How do we know what we know about God in our preaching and witness, and does it matter? Mike Ovey's chapter reminds us that, properly understood, theology is God's sharing of himself with us *truly* rather than our striving to master truth *exhaustively*.

The seven chapters following focus outwardly on the churches' responsibility to contend for the truth, relevance and goodness of the gospel as we seek to reach a lost world.

Part II

'The Priority of Truth' (Stefan Gustavsson) and 'Apologetics – Always Ready' (Kirsten Birkett) provide a compelling case for biblical apologetics and in so doing rescue this discipline from the false perception that it is a stuffy, extrabiblical enterprise for intellectuals.

In 'Gospel Cooperation Without Compromise' John Stevens presents a template for evangelical unity that captures the Bible's robust demands to uphold doctrine and ethics alongside its vision of visible unity around the gospel.

William Edgar's moving meditation, 'The Silence of God' is both a model of rich cultural engagement and a homage to Don Carson's love of all things French.

Part III

The evangelistic challenges and opportunities in reaching the world effectively are the focus of the final three chapters.

'Winning Hearts and Minds in a Secular Age' (Richard M. Cunningham) focuses on what is at stake, particularly for our children and young people, if evangelical leaders do not step up and work together to provide a compelling response to the secular vision for human flourishing.

Tim Keller and Michael Keller ('University Missions and Evangelism Today') draw on their considerable experience to outline the strategic rewards and challenges of university mission. They helpfully combine both the careful analysis and the practical responses required for us to be effective in this mission field.

John Piper's closing chapter, 'Doing Missions when Dying Is Gain', highlights both the urgency and the cost of intentionally taking the gospel to the world. Adolf von Harnack reputedly said that the early church 'out-lived, out-thought and out-died the pagans'. The preceding chapters have focused particularly on 'out-thinking'; this final chapter is a sobering and yet uplifting reminder that we are called to do all three.

Before leaving you to plunge into this stimulating volume, I should like to return to the piece written by Mike Ovey (former Principal of Oak Hill College): 'Is God the Only Theologian?'

Mike was one of the first authors I approached for a chapter and he knew straight away what he wanted to write about. He typically offered me generous encouragement, wise advice and mischievous suggestions for other chapters. Tragically, Mike died suddenly and unexpectedly on 7 January this year and leaves behind his wife, Heather, and their three children, Charlie, Harry and Ana. Mike was one of the finest theologians of his generation, but, more significantly, he was a loving husband, father and friend. It is a sad honour and privilege to publish posthumously his fine, albeit technical, chapter in this volume.

January 2017
Oxford, UK

Part I

1. PREACHING THAT CHANGES
THE CHURCH

David Jackman

There has been no shortage of men, ideas or movements over the past fifty years, whose common desire and motivation has been to change the church. Fashions come and go; experiments flourish and fade; yet any detached observer would surely be justified in concluding that the church, at least in the West, is still in a precarious state: often confused and distracted, seemingly lacking power, marginalized and ignored. It would be a bold (or perhaps naive) voice that claimed the church does not need to change.

Defining the Church

But what do we mean by 'the church'? Nearly fifty years ago, Martyn Lloyd-Jones was writing, 'Often one really has to ask about certain gatherings and communities of people whether they are entitled to the name church at all. The church so easily can degenerate into an organisation, or even, perhaps, into a social club or something of that kind.'[1] That has clearly not changed, even if those expressions of 'the church' have drastically diminished in size. But the aim of this chapter is not to discuss the doctrine of the church, which is far beyond its scope. Instead, we shall focus our discussion on 'the assembly of the firstborn who are enrolled in heaven', those who have come 'to the city of the living God, the heavenly Jerusalem' and 'to Jesus, the mediator of a new covenant, and to the sprinkled blood' (see Heb. 12:22–24).[2] This company of those redeemed through the sacrificial death of our Lord Jesus Christ consists of the church triumphant, in God's immediate presence, and of the church militant here on earth. This vast multitude, which no man can number and whose membership is known only to her head (2 Tim. 2:19), is expressed in time-and-space history both as the church universal and as the church local in each community where it has been planted. It is this company of believing people, gathered by the gospel, affirming the lordship of Christ, born again and indwelt by the Spirit of God that is the church we are concerned with. How does this 'church' need to change?

First, let us establish that we need have no fears for its continuance, whatever the attacks and challenges that it may face. 'I will build my church, and the gates of hell shall not prevail against it,' Jesus said (Matt. 16:18). Today we rejoice to be able still to affirm, with the apostle Paul, that the word of truth, the gospel, 'in the whole world . . . is bearing fruit and growing' (Col. 1:6). John Calvin's confidence has been amply confirmed over the past five hundred years, when he affirmed, 'God would not suffer his Church altogether to fall, having once founded it with the design of preserving it for ever; for he forsakes not the work of his own hands.' He commends to his readers this confidence, 'that the mutilated body of the Church, which is daily distracted, will be restored to its entireness; for God will not suffer his work to fail . . . The Church, though it may not always be in a flourishing condition, is ever safe and secure, and . . . God will miraculously heal it, as though it were a diseased body.'[3] During his earthly ministry our Lord healed many a diseased body by his powerful word and that is the means that he has provided for the healing and changing of his church.

Change Rooted in the Gospel

It is this concept of healing, breathing new life into the people of God, that lies at the heart of the change that needs constantly to be characteristic of both the church and of the individual believer. This roots the life of both the corporate community and the individual firmly in the gospel. For the gospel is about the greatest change of all: from darkness to light, from Satan to God, from death to life (see Col. 1:12–14). Moreover, the New Testament is clear that the new birth is the implantation of the seed of the life of the eternal God within his people, through his indwelling Spirit. These metaphors of birth and planting both imply growth and development, which are lifelong in this world and ultimately reach their fulfilment and completion in the life of the world to come. So Paul writes, 'I am sure of this, that he who began a good work in you will bring it to completion at the day of Jesus Christ' (Phil. 1:6). But also, in the same letter, he writes, 'Work out your own salvation with fear and trembling, for it is God who works in you' (Phil. 2:12–13). The changes that the church needs to experience are the changes of spiritual growth, of development to maturity, of the restoration of the image of God and of progressive transformation into the likeness of Christ. An increasingly godly church will produce an increasingly hungry world.

Distinctively Different

We need to remember that it has always been God's purpose that his people, bound to him by covenant grace, should become the light-bearers of divine truth to a broken world. That was the purpose and glory of the incarnation. 'The light shines in the darkness, and the darkness has not overcome it' (John 1:5). But that role had been assigned to Israel ('my firstborn son', Exod. 4:22) back in Deuteronomy 4:6–7:

> Keep them [God's statutes] and do them, for that will be your wisdom
> and your understanding in the sight of the peoples, who, when they
> hear all these statutes, will say, 'Surely this great nation is a wise and
> understanding people.' For what great nation is there that has a god
> so near to it as the LORD our God is to us, whenever we call upon him?

The distinctiveness of Israel's holy living was to be a testimony, for the glory of Israel's God, to the surrounding nations and a magnet to draw them to the uniqueness of Yahweh. In the face of Israel's failure, God promised an obedient servant through whom his promises to Abraham of blessing for all the families on earth would be fulfilled. 'I will make you as a light for the nations, that my salvation may reach to the end of the earth' (Isa. 49:6).

Not surprisingly, when the servant finally appears and begins to gather to himself a new covenant people of God, a new Israel, his kingdom manifesto instructs them, 'You are the salt of the earth . . . You are the light of the world. A city set on a hill cannot be hidden' (Matt. 5:13–14). These are all images of influence, of penetration. Further, 'let your light shine before others, so that they may see your good works and give glory to your Father who is in heaven' (Matt. 5:16). The unseen heavenly Father penetrates his world through the testimony and witness of the distinctly different, holy lives of his redeemed people. Such a church is 'fit for purpose'. Its very distinctiveness is a major means of the gospel's advance. Every act of pale conformity to the world's culture in which it is planted constitutes a denial of its purpose and a deprivation of its power. If the church is to fulfil the Great Commission to go into all the world to make disciples of all the nations it must authenticate the message by its own transformed character and diligent obedience to all that the Lord has commanded his people. What Christians are shouts so loudly that people do not hear what we say.

Growing in Godliness

We ought, therefore, to develop a clear biblical concept of the changes that need to happen in the church. These may include certain organizational, structural or presentational aspects, but they will not be the most significant areas. The apostles did not ignore issues of church order and governance, but what rings out again and again is their appeal for growth to godly maturity. In Ephesians 4, Paul describes his goal for the church as 'mature manhood . . . the measure of the stature of the fullness of Christ' (v. 13). And again, 'speaking the truth in love, we are to grow up in every way into him who is the head, into Christ' (v. 15). '[L]et us . . . go on to maturity' is the call of Hebrews 6:1. '[O]ne thing I do,' is Paul's personal testimony to the Philippians, 'forgetting what lies behind and straining forward to what lies ahead, I press on towards the goal for the prize of the upward call of God in Christ Jesus' (Phil. 3:13–14). This, then, is the change that matters most. It is the spiritual growth of the individual, and therefore by implication the sum of them all in the local congregation, into maturity. Like physical growth it is a process. It takes time, but it also takes nourishment and exercise. One of the most motivational verses in the New Testament, in my own experience, has been 2 Corinthians 3:18: 'And we all, with unveiled face, beholding the glory of the Lord, are being transformed into the same image from one degree of glory to another. For this comes from the Lord who is the Spirit.' As we do the 'beholding', the Spirit will accomplish the 'transforming'. It is a great promise. But how can it happen and, more especially, what is its relationship to preaching?

Significantly, the verse is set in the context of a longer passage about the ministry of the Spirit, the ministry of life, which is the stewardship God has committed to Paul and which he relates clearly to the preaching of the Word. This is even more obvious in another key passage in Colossians 1:25–29, which is a window into the innermost heart and motivation of the apostle. It is well worth quoting in full. Paul describes himself as

> a minister according to the stewardship from God that was given to me for you, to make the word of God fully known, the mystery hidden for ages and generations but now revealed to his saints. To them God chose to make known how great among the Gentiles are the riches of the glory of this mystery, which is Christ in you, the hope of glory. Him we proclaim, warning everyone and teaching everyone with all wisdom, that we may present everyone mature in Christ. For this I toil, struggling with all his energy that he powerfully works within me.

This is the heart of apostolic ministry received from the Lord himself and in this succession we are to take our stand too. The grand aim and objective is to bring all who are under this ministry to maturity (v. 28). The means for this is described as making 'the word of God fully known' (v. 25), which means not so much preaching through the whole Bible (though that would be a worthy aim in itself), but preaching Christ as the centre and key to all the Scriptures. 'Him we proclaim' (v. 28); that is, the Christ who is 'in you' in the present and who is 'the hope of glory' for the future (v. 27). The gospel is therefore not only the way in to the Christian life, but the way on as well. Paul's confidence is entirely in God, honouring his stewardship of the Word as he proclaims (a preaching Word) Christ in all his fullness, which is a major Colossians theme. This is proving to be hard work for Paul, as it always is for every preacher. He speaks about toil and struggle, which are both images of hard, back-breaking labour and expenditure of physical energy; but just as the focus of his content is on Christ, so the ability to keep doing this work is centred on the Holy Spirit who enables it to happen, powerfully working within him (v. 29). In summary, the apostolic confidence is that the Spirit of God takes the Word of God to accomplish the work of God. Perhaps we might add that there is no plan B!

The Key Role of Preaching

We now turn to the practical question of how this challenging but glorious task is to be accomplished. What sort of preaching will produce the desired change? Sadly, there are numerous failed models around, from which doubtless we can learn. In many contexts preaching is at a lamentably low ebb and expectations of anything better have been so eroded that there is frequently a desire to get rid of it altogether. It is outdated, outmoded and out of steam, we are told. But if we accept the authority of Scripture for the content of our faith, it is quite illogical not to accept its instruction about the methodology of its propagation. Proclamation is clearly central to God's purposes in and through the church and for the church's witness to the world.

Interestingly, the Bible is more concerned with the 'what' of preaching than with the 'how'. We should not be surprised that contemporary views of preaching reflect the norms of contemporary culture, whether in the preacher or in those who listen. In a recent interview, David Brooks, the American journalist and political commentator, identified the Western cultural shift of the last two decades as a move from self-effacement to the 'big me'. Consumer society teaches us that our desires are good and should be satisfied. We come 'to have a tremendous trust in them' and to pursue self-fulfilment at all costs. Social media exemplifies the self, broadcasting every detail of our lives and thoughts, building ourselves up, if not to win fame then at least to have followers.[4] Christians are not immune to these influences. We like to hear the sermons we like and often imagine that we can judge their value on that criterion alone. Preachers like to preach what is popular and to receive as much positive audience reaction as possible. Their greatest fear is that of offending the 'movers and shakers' in the congregation. They don't like controversy and don't want division. Indeed, their very positions and livelihood may depend upon keeping people happy. So there develops an unstated co-conspiracy between the preacher and the hearers, that nothing will ever be said beyond the bland and predictable. But, of course, this is a recipe for the status quo, or rather for a slow, but inevitable, decline in the spiritual welfare of the congregation. This kind of preaching does not change the church and so the church will not change the world.

The Bible in the Driving Seat

However skilful the communication, however impressive the technology, however exciting the presentation, if the Bible is not in the driving seat of the sermon there will be no lasting change of the sort that the New Testament sees as normal. So the important element is the content of the preaching. The contrast is between the Word of the Lord, which is living and enduring (1 Peter 1:23) and the word of the preacher, which at its best is flawed and transient. That may sound obvious, but it is very easy to slip away from that mooring. If Paul exhorted the Christians in Rome, 'Do not be conformed to this world, but be transformed by the renewal of your mind' (Rom. 12:2), what do you think he might say to us in our frenetic world of 24/7 communication, where the secular culture is continually seeking to conform us, with its myriad messages subtly undermining God's revealed truth? We need to be hearing God's Word, clearly explained, faithfully taught and engagingly applied every time we come together as the people of God. Because he is the speaking God, his people have always gathered together to hear and obey his Word. If that is not happening in that precious but short time that the preacher has each Sunday, then the world's insistent messages will win out and win us over to a compromised Christianity, which is no longer recognizably different from the mores of society at large. And if the church is neutralized in this way, then the strongest contemporary proof of the authenticity of the gospel has effectively been removed. Far from the church changing the world, the opposite will have happened.

The sort of preaching that changes the church is, in essence, expository. It takes the Bible seriously by putting it in the driving seat and allowing it to dictate the content of the sermon. That depends on a confidence in the authority, infallibility and sufficiency of the whole biblical revelation with regard to its contents. But it also involves a confidence in the power of the Word given to mediate a personal encounter with the living God. Both these elements must control the preacher in his preparation, if he is to prove a faithful messenger in his proclamation. God is the only ultimate author of Scripture, 'For no prophecy was ever produced by the will of man, but men spoke from God as they were carried along by the Holy Spirit' (2 Peter 1:21). But he is also the glorious subject of the reve-lation. We meet the author in his Word, since his purpose is to bring us into a deep personal knowledge of and fellowship with him, not merely to provide information about him. This is what is sometimes called the affective ingredient of preaching, since it involves the whole person – mind, heart and will – in response to God.[5]

Patterns of Preparation

The process of preparation for expository preaching necessarily involves all three ingredients. The expositor begins with a careful selection of the unit of the text he will be preaching, paying due attention to its length and context. Because of the wide-spread ignorance of Scripture today, even among Christians, many preachers seem to think that they must pack a sermon to bursting point and tend to choose passages that are too long for their congregations to cope with or benefit from. Let the Bible text determine the length of the unit, and where it is too long for one sermon, divide it into two. Other preachers veer in the opposite direction, taking perhaps just a verse and using it as a springboard to project themselves into all the doctrinal and ethical connections they can think of. These sermons may be fundamentally biblical in that they neither contradict nor misrepresent the teaching of Scripture, but they pay scant attention to the text in its context and end up as topical 'excursions', dependent on the ability of the preacher rather than the clarity of the Word. Once again, the preacher is in the driving seat. The problem then is the fulfilment of the old saying that 'a text without a context is a pretext for a proof text'.

I believe that the ideal pattern for a settled ministry in a local church context is to preach through a book of the Bible consecutively, unit by unit, giving due weight to the context of the whole book and the whole sweep of salvation history or biblical theology. In this way we learn and teach the Bible as God has given it to us, book by book, each of the sixty-six with its own unique content and purpose. The congregation will develop the same pattern for their own study and understanding of God's Word. An expository ministry will over time produce a Bible-loving, Bible-reading and, with prayer, Bible-obeying church. It has its own divinely given power to change. Of course, long books will need to be broken down into smaller units. A book like Isaiah might be better covered if it is divided into a number of shorter series, rather than our ploughing through from beginning to end. We need to be sensitive as to the stages and capabilities of our congregations, but we need always to be expounding the text, which we will handle rightly only when we set it its wider context.

Allowing the Text to Set the Agenda

We begin with the discipline of exegesis, where the question is 'What does the passage say?' It is a discipline because it is dependent on our careful listening to the text, becoming passionate hearers of God's Word before we become textual analysts. Of course, all the skills of exegetical analysis are vitally important here, but if our preaching is going to connect we need to hear God speaking directly to us personally, so that we understand the significance of the text that we must pass on to our hearers. This will lead to wider expository questions such as 'Why does the writer say it like this? Why

does he say it to these recipients and why at this point in his book?'
The 'what' is vitally important but without the deeper 'why' questions
it could merely produce an exegetical lecture, correct perhaps in
content but ineffective in producing change. So the exegetical work
always starts to open up further expository enquiry. And here the
golden key is context.

It is important to work on all three contexts in which every
biblical text finds its place. There is the immediate literary context
of what precedes and what follows the unit under consideration.
How does it fit the argument? Why is it needed at this stage? Next,
this relates to the wider context of the book, which explores what
the major themes of the book as a whole are and how this unit
connects to them. In turn, this raises the question of the book's
purpose, which could be described as the occasion of the composition, but which might be more helpfully identified as its pastoral
intention. If the whole Bible is God preaching God to us, what is
he saying about himself in this context and what was that designed
to achieve from the original recipients of the text? If we can discover
why this inspired word was given to 'them then', that will be of great
help in building the bridge to 'us now'. The third context is the
whole Bible where, comparing Scripture with Scripture, the unique
contribution of this unit will help us to grasp its distinctive contribution and, like any skilled craftsman, cut with the grain of the
wood. It will also ensure that we preach our text in the context of
the grace of God in the gospel and the centrality of Christ to the
whole revelation.

Preaching to the Whole Person

Context gives application. That is what enables the expositor to
connect with his hearers so that the nourishment of the text is
brought home to the life situation of the congregation. Of course,
that will involve all the purposes for which the Scripture was originally given: teaching, reproof, correction and training in righteousness
(2 Tim. 3:16). The appeal is to the mind to understand the truth, the
promises and encouragements as well as the commands and rebukes,
in order that the heart may receive it and be softened by it. The
default position of the sinful human heart is always to harden

against God's Word, which will happen quite naturally if the response that it was designed to achieve is neglected or resisted. The heart is the control centre of the personality. This is where our decisions are made, our priorities established, our life course set. So the greatest desire of the preacher is for the Word to travel through the mind to the heart in order to activate and energize the will, as it is put into practice in life. That is why he prays and prays. It is the Holy Spirit's gracious work to open blind eyes, to unstop deaf ears and to soften hard hearts. The preacher is to be faithful, to do the best job possible, but in glad recognition that, as Jesus said, 'apart from me you can do nothing' (John 15:5). This is hard work, consistently, week by week, but by prayer and the ministry of the Word (the apostolic priorities in Acts 6:4) the church is changed.[6]

The great value of preaching is that it can address all ages and stages in its presentation. People sometimes comment that many evangelical Bible churches are very middle class, but that could be because more attention is given to the Bible study groups or the one-to-one mentoring than to the public preaching of the Word. And yet it is preaching that builds the church as nothing else can. To feel at home in a Bible study group requires skills of reading, textual analysis, articulation and discussion of ideas which are the stuff of tertiary education, but may inadvertently exclude many. But anyone can listen to preaching, provided it is biblically clear and pastorally applied. When I was a pastor in Southampton I was privileged to see how the preached Word nurtured and grew the church, reaching the university professor and the boiler men from the city docks with equal effect, because beneath the external differences we are all sinners needing God's grace and saints under construction. The Word does the work. It has a power that is located nowhere else, simply because it is God's Word. '[I]t shall not return to me empty, but it shall accomplish that which I purpose, and shall succeed in the thing for which I sent it' (Isa. 55:11).

The Word Does the Work

Under consistent, consecutive exposition of the Scriptures, the church begins to change. Individuals start to understand why God says what he says. They begin to plumb 'the depth of the riches and wisdom and knowledge of God' (Rom. 11:33). They begin to see their connection to the worldwide family of God and the privilege of living their life for something that will last for ever. They begin to develop new priorities and to manage their personal resources differently. Family life is changed, as they submit to one another out of reverence for Christ. They begin to develop a biblically rigorous world view, as they experience the restoration of God's image in his people and recognize his sovereignty in every situation in his world.

Evangelism also receives a new impetus, when church members begin to grow in likeness to the Lord Jesus and reflect his light into the multitude of situations where God has placed them. It has been said that what the gospel needs is not slick salesmen, but more free samples. We should never underestimate the power of a consistent, godly life to witness to the truth of the gospel and introduce others to the Saviour. Sadly, the corollary is also true. So many are caused to stumble by the inconsistency of Christian profession, when the realities of godly maturity are not evident in our personal relationships. Evangelism is overflow of the life within (John 7:37–39) but that life is nurtured and developed only as the people of God are fed by faithful preachers who rightly handle the word of truth (2 Tim. 2:15).

The greatest way in which the church needs to change is to regain our confidence in the power of God's Word, a cause to which Don Carson has devoted his life unstintingly and to such great effect, for which we thank and praise God. We need to pray for a new generation of biblical expositors around the world who will give their lives to stating, explaining and applying God's powerful Word. That requires the conviction expressed recently by Tim Keller in his book on preaching:

> The Bible does not say that God speaks and then proceeds to act, that he names and then proceeds to shape – but that God's speaking and acting are the same thing. His Word is his action, his divine power . . . if you believe that the preaching of the Word is one of the main channels of God's action in the world, then with great care and confidence you will uncover the meaning of the text fully expecting that God's Spirit will act in listeners' lives.[7]

The task will never be complete this side of heaven, but there can be no greater privilege than to have a part, however small, in the divine plan that galvanizes the whole creation. The watchword of the Reformation is still true: 'The reformed church is always to be reformed.' And so is its less well-known conclusion: 'according to the Word of God'. In fact, there is no other resource that will enable this to happen. Speaking of God's development project, which is the church, in his comments on Ephesians 5:25–27, John Calvin writes, 'The Lord is daily smoothing its wrinkles and wiping away its spots. Hence it follows that its holiness is not yet perfect. Such, then, is the holiness of the church; it makes daily progress, but it is not yet perfect; it daily advances, but as yet has not reached the goal.'[8] Let us pray that in our time, with all its confusion and turmoil, God will raise up an army of fearless preachers whose ministries of persistent dedication and faithfulness to the exposition of the Scriptures will change first the church and then the world.

Notes

1. D. Martyn Lloyd-Jones, *Preaching and Preachers* (London: Hodder & Stoughton, 1971), p. 10.

2. Bible quotations in this chapter are from the English Standard Version.

3. John Calvin, *Commentary on the Book of Psalms*, vol. 5 (Grand Rapids, Mich.: Baker, 1979), pp. 293–294, quoted in W. Robert Godfrey, *Reformation Sketches* (Phillipsburg, N.J.: Presbyterian & Reformed, 2003), p. 76.

4. Interview on *Catholic News Agency*, 21 May 2015 <http://www.catholicnewsagency.com>.

5. For a valuable treatment of this important theme, see Josh Moody and Robin Weekes, *Burning Hearts: Preaching to the Affections* (Fearn: Christian Focus, 2014).

6. For further practical help, see the video course 'Equipped to Preach the Word' <http://www.proctrust.org.uk/equipped>.

7. *Christianity Today*, 26 October 2015, introducing Tim Keller, *Preaching* (London: Hodder & Stoughton, 2015).

8. John Calvin, *Institutes of the Christian Religion*, 4.1.17, quoted on 'Grace to You' blog, 29 August 2011 <http://www.gty.org>.

2. PREACHER AND THEOLOGIAN: THE IDEAL CHRISTIAN COMMUNICATOR

J.I. Packer

I was startled when asked, in my tenth decade and just after macular degeneration had set in, to write for this seventieth-birthday book for the redoubtable Don Carson, and my first (reluctant) thought was that on grounds of age and health I should decline. What I offer now is a revision of a piece that I wrote more than twenty years ago. It hammers a point that was true then, is true today, and will stay true until the Lord comes back, namely that to be useful pastoral preachers need a theological frame along with exegetical and applicatory skills. Don, I am sure, will agree. Happy birthday!

* * *

It is widely imagined that one can fulfil the preacher's role without being a theologian. This thought is of a piece with the idea that one can fulfil the theologian's role without being a preacher. I should like to assault both notions together, for both are perverse; but you cannot kick with two feet simultaneously, and in any case the title which I have chosen limits me to countering the first. So here I aim simply to show how needful it is for a preacher to be a theologian.

Theology

At the start of each academic year at Regent College all professors used to be asked to strut a few minutes of their stuff for the orientation of incoming students. I regularly began my bit of the programme by declaring myself to be a servant of the Queen – that is, of theology, the true queen of the sciences; and then I gave a sort of Identikit profile of the lady who commands my allegiance. I referred to her *sight*, explaining that she has to wear glasses, since she can see nothing clearly till she looks at it through the lens of Holy Scripture. I spoke of her *shape*, indicating that she has a graceful – that is, a grace-full – figure, which she works to keep by devotional and doxological habits of God-centred thinking. And I said that she is *sassy* – which is old-American for *saucy*, and signifies a perkiness that Americans admire (not as it was in the England of my youth, where *sauce* meant *cheek*, and 'None of your sauce!' was an ultimate put-down). I defined the sassiness of theology as an unwillingness to keep quiet when God was regularly misrepresented and revealed truth is put in jeopardy. Then I urged that these character qualities should appear in all the Queen's servants, particularly those who plan to preach. Thus I sought to prepare our freshers for their coming studies.

Pursuing the picture, as I would do in their first theology class, we may truly say that though the Queen is not always ideally clad in public, when she is she is most impressive. Truth, wisdom, devotion, breadth, clarity and practicality are then the leading motifs of her ensemble, and the ensemble itself consists of ten linked disciplines, Bible-based and mutually supportive. The first is *exegesis*, for which the question always is, 'What was this or that biblical text written to convey to its readers?'[1] The second is *biblical theology*, for which the question is, 'What is the teaching of this or that book, and the total message of the canonical books on this or that subject?' The third is *historical theology*, the bonding glue of church history, exploring how Christians in the past viewed specific biblical truths. The fourth is *systematic theology*, which rethinks biblical theology with the help of historical theology in order to restate the faith, topic by topic and as a whole, in relation to current interests, assumptions, questions, hopes, fears and uncertainties in today's church and world. The fifth is *apologetics*, which seeks to commend and defend the faith as rational and true in the face of current unbelief, misbelief and puzzlement. The sixth is *ethics*, which systematizes the standards of Christian life and conduct and applies them to particular cases. The seventh is *spiritual theology*, sometimes called devotional or ascetic theology or Christian spirituality, which studies how to understand and maintain sanctifying communion with God. The eighth is *missiology*, which aims to see how God's people should view and tackle their gospel-spreading, church-planting and welfare-bringing tasks across cultural barriers worldwide. The ninth is *liturgy*, which asks how God is best and most truly worshipped, and how true worship may be achieved in existing churches. The tenth is *practical theology*, embracing pastoral theology, family theology and political theology as it explores how to further God's work and glory in home, church and society.

Full-dressed as distinct from half-dressed theology, if I may put it so, will show competence in all these disciplines. Theology is often described as a quadrilateral of biblical, historical, theological and practical studies, but the ten-discipline analysis is more precise.[2] Theological education latches on to it, and constructs its syllabi accordingly.

The focus of the Queen's outfit is systematic theology, which draws its raw material from the first three disciplines and serves the church by providing resources of digested truth for the last six. It is called *systematic* not because it works by building up speculative inferences about God, or by scaling him down so as to dissolve away the mystery of his being and render him manageable by our finite minds (both those procedures would falsify his reality), but because it takes all the truths, visions, valuations and admonitions with which the Holy Spirit feeds the church through the Scriptures and seeks to think them together in a clear, coherent and orderly way. It separates out seven main topical fields – revelation; God; man; Christ; the Holy Spirit; the church; the future[3] – and fills in all that Scripture is found to say about each. In the past this discipline was called *dogmatic theology* and given the task of analysing, crystallizing and where necessary recasting those biblical truths that the church has committed itself in credal and confessional statements to uphold and teach. The description derives not from dogmatism and rigidity as a personal style among theologians (perish the thought!) but from *dogma*, a Greek word meaning that which has been decided. *Systematic*, however, seems to me the better label, both because integrated spelling out of revealed truth as such is the goal and because everything taught in the Bible is theology's business, whether or not the church's creeds include it.

Systematic theology moves between, and regularly blends, three styles of thought and speech, each of which needs separate appreciation for the job it does. These are the *kerygmatic*, exploring in comprehensive terms the question 'What is the Bible telling us?'; the *confessional*, exploring in contemporary terms, with all sorts of interactions, the question 'How should the church assert this so as to be heard?'; and the *philosophical*, exploring in logical terms the question 'What is the exact meaning of these biblical and churchly affirmations?' For success in the first mode, listening to the Bible is all-important; for success in the second mode, listening to the world is what matters; for success in the third mode, listening to the technicians of language and communication is what counts. Still pursuing our parable, we could describe these three styles as the three-tone colour scheme of the Queen's dress. We should note that theology's technical terms mostly belong to styles two and three, where their role is to highlight the gems displayed in essentially biblical language by style one.

The fact that systematic theology provides the raw material for disciplines five to ten as listed above shows clearly enough that systematic theology is to the church's health as diet is to the body's health: health suffers if what is ingested is not right. All aspects of practical Christianity will be weakened if 'systematics' is neglected. Christian history has seen many movements of experience-oriented reaction against theology's supposedly barren intellectualism. These movements have thought they could get on without serious theological study, and have discouraged their adherents from engaging in it. In the short term, while living on theological capital brought in from outside by their founders, they have often channelled spiritual life in an impressive way, but with the passage of time they have again and again lapsed into old errors and forms of imbalance and stuntedness that, for lack of theological resources, they are unable effectively to correct, and that prompt the rest of the church to stand back from them. 'No one ever tried to break logic but what logic broke him' is a dictum ascribed to A.S. Pringle-Pattison;[4] something similar has to be said about systematic theology.

The above portrayal of the Queen of the sciences is, of course, ideal. In practice, systematic theologians often fall short through overlooking or disregarding biblical data, or handling it in terms of some distorting paradigm of understanding or of truth that is abroad in either the church or the world or both. There are only three methods of procedure, fundamentally speaking, in theological work: the one we have surveyed, which I call *biblicist*; that which appeals to supposedly infallible pronouncements by the church as the ultimate standard, a method that I call *traditionalist*; and the procedure which, having reviewed the deliverances of Scripture and the history of Christian thought by the light of contemporary secular opinions, treats the dictates of the theologian's reason, conscience or immediate religious awareness as God's truth for that time, a method that I call *subjectivist*. No one can study theology without coming to regard two of those three as radically wrong; but any of them can be adulterated by inconsistent slidings from time to time at the level of method. So, with God's help, self-assessment (in terms of our bit of whimsy, the Queen examining herself in the mirror of Holy Scripture) and self-reformation (the Queen tidying herself as the mirror shows she needs to do) are regularly required of those who, correctly, follow the biblicist method as best they can. I say 'as best they can' because we should not expect ever in this world to reach a point where the church and the Christian have nothing more to set straight or to take in at convictional level; such perfection is for heaven, and is not given here.

But here and now we all need the best theology we can get. Every time we mention God we become theologians, and the only question is whether we are going to be good ones or bad ones. And this touches both thought and life. Older writers affirmed, and our ten-discipline analysis showed, that theology is a 'theoretico-practical' study – 'the science of living blessedly for ever',[5] as William Perkins, the Puritan, breathtakingly defined it. As a critical and analytical exploration of the evidence of revelation about reality (God, and life under God), and as a developed intellectual organism interpreting and prescribing for the human condition according to its own insight into reality, theology may well be called a science, with a life enriched by God as its end-product. It moves to that end-product in two stages.

First, it leads to a deeper understanding of the Bible, by giving us an ordered overview of what is demonstrably in the Bible and so telling us what to look for in the Bible. When my wife and I walk in the country, she sees far more than I do, not because her eyes work better than mine, but because she is a naturalist who recognizes birds, trees, plants, little animals and much more when she sees them. I, by contrast, see without understanding – without observing, as Sherlock Holmes expressed it in his criticism of Dr Watson. To be sure, the boot is on the other foot when we inspect old-fashioned steam railway locomotives: all my wife knows is that they are water-boilers on wheels, self-propelled; but I, who once hoped to be an engine-driver, know more about them than that, and consequently see more of what I am looking at than she does. The point is that prior theoretical knowledge enables you to observe more of what is there. In Bible study, the theologically unaware are likely to overlook the significance of what they read; which is why Calvin tailored the second and subsequent editions of his *Institutes* as a preparation for exploring the Scriptures themselves.[6] In this he may have shown more wisdom than do some of the theorists of what is called nowadays 'inductive Bible study', who tell you to 'observe' without giving you any theological orientation to help you do it.

Since the Reformation the cardinal principle of biblical interpretation among Protestants has been *Sacra Scriptura sui ipsius interpres* – the Holy Scripture is its own interpreter, interpreting itself. The assumption is that proper interpretation will bring out a rational coherence and consistency that are already there in the text, since it all comes from a single divine mind, and God the Holy Spirit can be trusted not to have contradicted himself in masterminding the writing of the sixty-six books. The assumption is valid and the method is right, but we shall still get along far faster if we have available a catechetical-level theology, that is, a crystallized and digested overview of biblical teaching as a whole, with the main emphases brought out, that will help us to see what we are looking at in each biblical passage. Especially is this so with regard to biblical statements about God, where each noun, adjective and verb that is used of God – that is, that God, the primary author of the text, uses of himself – bears a sense that at points differs to a degree from its sense when used of humans. The appropriate adjustment for us to make in each case is to drop the associations of finitude and moral limitation that all words used of humans naturally carry, and replace them with notions of the infinite self-existence and moral glory that some texts ascribe to God explicitly. Inductive Bible study would doubtless make one aware of the need for this adjustment as one kept comparing Scripture with Scripture over the years, but to have theology make it explicit and drill one in it from the start advances one's understanding more quickly. From this standpoint, to speak of theology as the science of Bible study is both true and illuminating.

Secondly, theology teaches us how to apply revealed truth for the leading of our lives; thus theology guides our steps, grants us vision and fuels our worship, while at the same time disinfecting our minds from the inadequate, distorted and corrupt ideas of God and godliness that come naturally to our fallen intellect. These ideas, if not correct, will mislead us and hold us back, and perhaps totally derail us, in our Christian practice, and will certainly be a stumbling-block to those whom we seek to help. Before you can become a physician or a garage mechanic you need a thorough theoretical grounding, in the one case in physiology and pathology, in the other in the mechanisms and maintenance of cars, and without it you would inevitably do damage – perhaps a great deal of damage. Similarly, we need a proper theoretical grounding in the life of faith and obedience before we can either live that life consistently ourselves or help anyone else to do so. Guided by theology, however, we may start to experience 'living blessedly for ever' in peace, hope, joy and love Godward, and be able to help others into that same supernaturalized existence.

These enrichments to which theology leads are crucial for all Christians, but particularly for preachers, as we shall see.

Preaching

A theological account of theology, formally viewed, is now before us. In this section a similar account of preaching will be set beside it.

What is preaching? Sociologically and institutionally, preaching has to be defined in terms of pulpits and pews, meetings and programmes, and corporate expectations fulfilled more or less by the monologue of a stated leader. Our biblical and theological approach, however, leads to a definition in terms of divine purpose rather than human performance. The definition comes out thus: preaching is incarnational communication from God, prophetic, persuasive and powerful – that is, power-full. Let me explain.

First, preaching is *communication*. God, our Maker and Redeemer, is constantly speaking his word to the human race, and within it particularly to his own believing people. That word is his message of grace to sinners, which he spoke definitively in and through the Christ-centred revelatory and redemptive process that the Bible records, and now speaks definitively in and through the biblical record itself. God makes himself known by telling us specific things about himself and about ourselves in relation to him, and thus he invites and draws us into repentance, faith, love and new life in restored friendly fellowship with himself. The text of the Bible, which from this standpoint may properly be described as God preaching to us, is the primary form of this communication, and the messages of preachers who faithfully relay the elements of God's total message constitute its derivative form. Jesus Christ, the Son of God incarnate, crucified, risen, ascended, reigning and returning, is the focal centre of God's communication; the new-covenant relationship between God and ourselves through Christ is its immediate announced objective; and the sanctifying of all life under Christ to the glory of God and the blessing of humanity is its ultimate goal. Preachers are only preachers, that is, messengers of God, so far as they understand these things, keep them in sight and make them the staple substance of their own messages. Pulpiteers who deliver anything different or anything less are failing to communicate God's message, and that means they are not preachers in the theological sense of that word. No doubt they intend to be, but they do not succeed.

Secondly, preaching is *prophetic* communication. The prophets of Bible times were God's spokesmen and sounding boards. They passed on oracular and visionary messages, admonitory, hortatory and revelatory, that God had given them: they were not sources, but channels. The Christian preacher must function in the same way. To be sure, he will do it in a didactic mode, like the apostles, who spoke as God-taught teachers, rather than in the dualistic mode of the prophets, whose ministry of instruction was limited to faithfulness as God's messenger boys, whom he could trust to deliver his oracles word for word. But in making it his business to confront people not with his own ideas, as such, but with the contents of the Word of God, the Christian preacher will show himself to stand in the prophetic succession. The words of the man who preaches must carry the word of the God who speaks.

It thus appears that all true preaching is biblical interpretation – that is, elucidation and application of 'God's Word written'.[7] Preaching means speaking God's own message in his name, that is, as his representative; and this is possible for us, with our sin-twisted minds, only as we labour faithfully to echo, restate and reapply God's once-for-all witness to himself in Holy Scripture. Biblical interpretation means theological exegesis of the text, in relation to the rest of the organism of revealed truth, for the scripturally defined purposes of teaching, discernment of our defects, correction and training in righteousness (see 2 Tim. 3:16–17). Such applicatory interpretation chimes in with the nature and purpose of all the canonical books as their human authors conceived them, and is in fact the most faithful and right-minded handling of them that can be imagined. It is worth pausing to illustrate this.

In their character as God's mouthpieces the prophets proclaimed, and then wrote down, messages that were essentially God's appeals to Israel for repentance, righteousness, fidelity and true worship. Christians' hearts are to be searched by them, just as were the hearts of Old Testament saints and sinners, and true preachers will apply them so.

In their role as Christ's commissioned agents and ambassadors (see 2 Cor. 5:20), the apostles wrote letters of exhortation and direction – epistolary sermons – to keep Christians on track. God means them to do that job for us today, and true preachers will use them accordingly.

The Old Testament historians, whom the Jews perceptively called the former prophets, told of God's dealings with people and nations in a way that was clearly meant to evoke praise and teach lessons

about faith and obedience on the one hand, and unbelief and dis-
obedience on the other. These lessons were meant to mould and
shape readers' lives for God, and true preachers today will enforce
them to that end.

The Gospels prove on inspection to be not artless memoirs of
Jesus (as was once thought), but four careful selections of stories
about his sayings, doings and sufferings, all so arranged and angled
that 'the gospel' – the life-changing news of a divine Saviour – will
leap out into the thoughtful reader's mind and heart. True preachers
will bring this out, and spend their strength to make it happen.

The wisdom books (of which it was well said that the Psalms
teach us how to praise, the Proverbs how to live, the Song of
Solomon how to love, Job how to endure and Ecclesiastes how to
enjoy) are didactic preaching in substance, and should be expounded
accordingly.

So we might go on. When Paul said that 'everything that was
written in the past was written to teach us, so that through . . . the
encouragement of the Scriptures we might have hope' (Rom. 15:4),[8]
his thought was that God meant all the Old Testament books to
function in due course as his own preaching to Christians. So the
Bible itself must preach, and must be seen and felt to preach, in all
our preaching. The Westminster Directory for Public Worship was
right to require preachers, when raising a point from a text, to labour
to let their hearers see 'how God teaches it from thence'[9] – in other
words, to show that it is being read out of the sacred text, not read
into it. This is the true prophetic dimension of preaching.[10]

Thirdly, preaching is *persuasive* communication. Persuasion in a
good cause expresses both respect for others as rational beings and
concern for their welfare, as persons not yet fully abreast of the way
of truth and wisdom. Persuasion was how Paul defined his evangelistic ministry ('we try to persuade . . . We implore . . . we urge'; 2 Cor.
5:11, 20; 6:1), and persuasion was how Luke described it (Acts 18:4;
19:8; 28:23). Though the Bible is clear that hearts are changed, and
faith and faithfulness generated, only by the new-creating power of
God, it is equally clear that persuasion is the means we are meant to
use if changed lives are what we want to see. Christian persuasion
is a matter of giving reasons, factual and prudential, for embracing
the belief and behaviour that constitute discipleship to Jesus Christ,

and then of pressing God's commands, promises, warnings and assurances, with a view to winning one's hearer or hearers (or, if it is being done by writing, one's readers) to a positive response. Preaching is not bludgeoning and browbeating, but persuading. The latter is its only proper style, the path of patent and patient love.

Fourthly, preaching is *power-full* communication. The reference here is not to loud shouting, pulpit-beating for emphasis, or any other display of animal energy, but to the way God is pleased to link the ministry of the Holy Spirit with the ministry of the Word, so that the preached message pierces hearers' hearts. Paul speaks of this when he says that at Corinth, where people expected him as a travelling pundit to show off his learning, and where he had resolved to stick to 'the testimony about God ... Jesus Christ and him crucified', '[m]y message and my preaching were not with wise and persuasive words [he is being ironic, and means 'frivolously captivating'; he is not contradicting 2 Cor. 5:11!], but with a demonstration of the Spirit's power, so that your faith might not rest on men's wisdom, but on God's power' (1 Cor. 2:1–5). The assumption reflected here is that, other things being equal, the Holy Spirit will give the preacher a gift of understanding and utterance that will cause the word spoken to make a spiritual impact and bring forth spiritual fruits. In experience, other things are not always equal. The preacher's message, heart, life and approach to the particular preaching situation may be insufficiently Christ-centred and bad in a number of ways. He may fail to be clear, or to commend himself credibly as a serious and humble servant of Jesus Christ. He may have grown proudly self-reliant, and neglected to pray for his preaching. If he comes across as a mechanical formalist whose heart is not in his communicating, or as a self-absorbed, manipulative and untrustworthy person, or as a play-actor indulging in unreality with his pulpit dramatics and rhetoric, no spiritual impact is likely. Factors in the hearers as well as in the speaker may also quench the Spirit. But where the Spirit is unquenched the power of God will be present to work with and through the Word, and an impact will be made for God.

Fifthly, preaching is *incarnational* communication. Phillips Brooks indicated this when he declared that preaching is truth through personality; though 'personhood', I think, would express his thought more precisely. The point is that the preacher is inescapably part of the message. He must model by his demeanour both the authority of the truths he is communicating and the response to them that he seeks to evoke. There is no substitute for this: spiritual reality in the sense defined is a 'must'. Preachers should seek it, but only their hearers will know if they have found it. Without it, however, preaching in the theological sense does not occur, and so the speaker's post-sermon question 'Did I *preach?*' becomes a necessary enquiry.

Preacher and Theologian

Having seen, at least in formal theological outline, what theology and preaching essentially are, I can now develop the point towards which I have been driving from the start, namely that a preacher needs to be a theologian of some competence in order to do his job.

I make here a number of assumptions. The first is that the preacher is a congregational leader, recognized as such, to whom people look as an embodiment of true Christianity, and whose preaching is heard as setting standards for himself and his hearers alike. The second is that his role makes him the principal agent in the theological and spiritual formation of those to whom he regularly preaches, and that he is answerable to God for the strategy of teaching and application that he pursues as a means to that end. The third is that teaching with application – preaching, that is – in a worship context is the main means of a congregation's spiritual formation, whatever other occasions and modes of instruction may be programmed into its life. The fourth is that the anti-intellectual thrust of pietisms in the church and relativisms in the world has left twenty-first-century congregations, and the Christians who make them up, much less concerned about doctrinal truth than they need to be, so that a conscience about and an appetite for learning the Word of God have to be created. The fifth is that all members of all modern Western congregations are constantly confronted by deviant opinions and value systems, such as the anti-Christianity of Jehovah's Witnesses, Mormons, Islam and the New Age, the out-of-shape Christianity of Roman Catholicism, the watered-down, indeed washed-out, Christianity of Protestant liberalism, and the post-Christian hedonism, materialism and cynicism projected by the media and movies, and the books, plays, newspapers, magazines, schools, universities and politicians that combine to become opinion-makers for tomorrow; and Christians have to be taught how to resist the brainwashing impact of these aberrations. The present-day preacher faces a formidable task of adult Christian education, and must plan his pulpit strategy in a way that will teach discrimination in the face of deviation and fortitude in holding fast to truth. It will not suffice, in an age like ours, for sermons to be isolated utterances, however noble each might be: they need to form a syllabus, covering the whole waterfront of challenges to revealed truth as well as the full landscape of the truth itself. Whether the sermons are announced in syllabus terms is not important; what matters is that the preacher should be facing up to his instructional and formational responsibility, and preaching according to his own thought-out strategy for discharging it.

My submission is that he cannot hope to meet this requirement completely unless he knows his way around in the fields of systematic theology, apologetics, ethics and spiritual life. He needs to be well versed in the implications of a God-centred view of this created world and life within it. He needs to be deeply knowledgeable about the damage done to humanity's thought-life and moral nature by sin, the anti-God allergy in our fallen make-up that controls our pre-regenerate existence. He needs a thorough understanding of God's plan of salvation through Jesus Christ the mediator and of the regenerating work of the Holy Spirit in its intellectual, volitional, emotional and transformational aspects. He needs to be especially clear on what is involved in the authentic Christian life of faith, repentance, hope, love, self-denial, humility, dependence, and pleasing and worshipping and glorifying God; the life of faithful perseverance under pressure and of sustained spiritual warfare against the world, the flesh and the devil; the life of prayer to, and fellowship with, the Father and the Son; the life of sanctification and service, adoration and assurance, through the inward ministry of the Holy Spirit. He must know, and be able to show, what is involved, not only at the centre but also at the edges, in maintaining biblical standards, attitudes and lifestyle distinctives in a world of competing religions and ideologies on the one hand and rampant irreligion and demoralization on the other. Amid all the cross-currents of our tempest-tossed culture he must be able to communicate in and through his expositions – that is, to let the Bible communicate through him – a sustained vision of a consistent, tri-umphant, God-fearing and God-honouring Christian life. I venture to affirm that if he is not something of a theologian, permanently apprenticed to the ten disciplines listed earlier because he sees them as fundamental to the pastoral life, the task will prove to be far beyond him.

For, in the first place, only theology as described will secure for our preaching *adequacy of coverage*. All we who preach have our favourite themes on which we like to harp, and our areas of chronic neglect where, because our interest is less, we are tempted to leave the necessary thinking and teaching to somebody else. But the pastoral preacher's mandate, like Paul's, is 'to proclaim . . . the whole will [counsel, plan, purpose, intention, requirement] of God' (Acts 20:27). The substance and thrust of our sermons must come not only from personal vision and excitement about an old war-horse theme or a recent enthusiasm, plus our general sense of what might do some people some good, but from our focused knowledge of the range of revealed truth as well. We must know what are the fundamentals, the trunk and main branches of the Christian doctrinal tree: the sovereignty of God in creation, providence and grace; the trinitarian specifics of the Apostles' Creed; justification by faith alone through Christ's substitutionary atonement; sal-vation by grace alone through the regenerating work of the Holy Spirit; the centrality of the church in the Father's purposes; the coming return of Christ to judgment; and the certainty that heaven's glory or hell's misery will be everyone's final destiny. These funda-mentals must be faithfully and thoroughly taught, just as the basic principles of our spiritual life at home, in the church and in the world must be. Countering mistaken notions as one goes along and showing that Christianity is a faith that has reason on its side are further elements in the preacher's task; how much of this is done on each occasion will depend on the text and the preacher's judge-ment of what the congregation needs, but though incidental it is very much part of the agenda. I should state explicitly that in saying these things I have in view not topical theological lectures in the pulpit – that, to my mind, could never be right – but rather biblical expository sermons, appropriately angled. Unless our preparation for regular preaching includes regular theological study, however, the above specifications are unlikely to be met. We who preach might well examine ourselves on this point before going further with the argument.

In the second place, only theology as described will secure *accuracy of exposition*. The story of the unskilled preacher who took the text '[H]ow shall we escape if we neglect such a great salvation?' (Heb. 2:3), and announced that his headings would be (1) the greatness of the salvation and (2) hints for escaping if we neglect it, has a warning for us here. Exposition must be accurate. Because the preacher shows what the text means for us today, and does not stop short at what it meant for its first readers, he rather than the academic commentator is the true interpreter of the Bible. But we reach the present-day meaning via the historical meaning, and while inductive exegesis of the text in its context is the finally authoritative method for achieving this, systematic theology, which is a digest of the findings of generations of Bible students, will constantly point us in the right direction. Donald Macleod thus comments on the description of Jesus Christ, God's Son, as 'the firstborn of all creation' (Col. 1:15, ESV), 'All that the church learned in the Arian controversy forbids us to tolerate any exegesis that compromises either the pre-existence or the deity (creator-hood) of the Savior,'[11] and he is right. To be sure, the references in the letter itself to all the fullness of God being in Christ (1:19; 2:9) confirm the wrongness of the Arian exegesis, which made the Son the first and noblest of the creatures, called 'Son' as an honorific courtesy title; but guidance in this matter from seventeen centuries of text-tested theology is not to be sneezed at.

Macleod gives a further example:

the notorious crux, Hebrews 6:4ff.: 'For it is impossible for those who were once enlightened and have tasted the heavenly gift and been made partakers of the Holy Spirit and have tasted the good word of God and the powers of the age to come, if they fall away, to renew them to repentance.' Prima *facie* this passage suggests that true believers can commit apostasy. Dogmatics alerts us, however, to the fact that such an interpretation is untenable, and closer examination of the passage itself confirms that it is pointing in the direction of another doctrine altogether – the doctrine of temporary faith.[12]

So we might go on, if there was need. As a guide in, and a check on, exegesis, theology can be invaluable.

There are areas of revealed truth that confront us starkly with the incomprehensible mystery of God's being and ways. In these areas the basic biblical conceptions are not always easy to hold on to, and it is very easy to mishandle texts that embody them. If, for instance, we lack a biblical understanding of the Trinity, one that avoids tritheism on the one hand and Sabellianism (God is one person playing three roles in one story, like the late Peter Sellers) on the other, we are not likely to be accurate in our handling of texts that speak of God's plan of salvation, the team job in which Father, Son and Holy Spirit work together to bring sinners to glory; nor are we likely to deal accurately with texts on the transactional reality of the atonement, the Son's offering himself to the Father through the Spirit to bear the penalty due to us for our sins.

Or if we lack a biblical understanding of God's upholding of us as free and responsible decision-makers while overruling all our thoughts and actions according to his own will as to what shall be, we are not likely to deal accurately with texts about our life in Christ, where self-reliant activism is ruled out and God-dependent activity is to be the pattern, where the faith we exercise is the gift of God, where the indwelling Spirit energizes moral effort, and where we live and obey in awe and reverence, knowing that it is God who works in us to make us will and act as he wants us to do.

These are sample spheres of reality in which we need the help of theology to achieve exposition that is accurate and precise.

In the third place, only theology as described will secure *adequacy of application* when we preach. Theology offers a ready-made grid for making applications, and this is help that we need, for the theory of application is not on the whole well understood. The rhetoric, style and technique of application will of course vary from preacher to preacher, but the activity of application as such has an unvarying logic, which we can state thus: If this principle is truth from God, what difference should it make to our thinking, our resolves, our

emotional attitudes, our motivation and our view of our own
spiritual state at this moment? More fully: if this principle is truth
that God teaches and guarantees, then the following questions arise:

1. What particular judgements, and ways of thinking, does
   it require of us, and what habits of mind and particular
   opinions does it forbid us to entertain, and charge us
   to change if they are part of our life at present?
   (This is application to the mind.)
2. What particular actions, and what types of virtuous
   behaviour, does it require of us, and what vicious acts
   and habits does it forbid, and tell us to renounce herewith?
   (This is application to the will.)
3. What does it teach us to love, desire, hope for, insist on
   and rejoice in, and what does it direct us to hate, abhor,
   fear, shrink from and be sad at? (This is application to those
   emotionally freighted dispositional attitudes that the Puritans
   called 'affections'.)[13]
4. What encouragements are there here to embrace
   righteousness, or a particular aspect of righteousness, and
   persevere in it, and what discouragements are there here
   to dissuade us from lapsing into sinful habits and actions?
   (This is application at the level of motivation.)
5. How do we measure up to the requirements of this truth
   at this moment? And what are we going to do about our
   present shortcomings here, as self-scrutiny reveals them?
   And what conformity to the truth's requirements do we find
   in ourselves, for which we ought to thank God? And how
   do we propose to maintain and increase that conformity?
   (This is application for self-knowledge and self-assessment,
   as a step towards salutary adjustments of our life.)[14]

Clearly, not all the possible applications of each truth to all the
different sorts of people one thinks one is preaching to (formalists,
seekers, the self-righteous, the self-despairing, young Christians,
veteran Christians, struggling Christians, and so on) can be made in
every sermon, or it would never end! But the Puritans, the all-time
specialists in application, gave something like half their preaching

time to this task, and when one is preparing an expository sermon that is a good rule of thumb.

Comparison with the Puritans, the pioneer evangelicals, and expositors like J.C. Ryle and Arthur Pink, will soon convince us that the applicatory aspect of pastoral preaching today is underdeveloped. One reason for this is that in an age like ours, in which the Scriptures are not well known or well respected, we are preoccupied with communicating biblical content and vindicating its divine authority, so that searching applications get crowded out. But a deeper reason is that, lacking a full-scale biblical and theological understanding of the Christian life – a systematic spirituality, as we might call it – we simply do not see what applications need to be made. Yet application is crucially important, partly because without it the preached Word will not humble and change people, and partly because it is in the process of application, as the Word is brought home to search the heart, that the sense of its divine authority becomes strongest and the habit of submitting to it is most thoroughly formed. So the Westminster Directory was right to declare that the preacher

> is not to rest in general doctrine ... but to bring it home to special
> use, by application to his hearers: which albeit it prove a work of great
> difficulty to himself, requiring much prudence, zeal, and meditation,
> and to the natural and corrupt man will be very unpleasant; yet he is to
> endeavour to perform it in such a manner, that his auditors may feel the
> word of God to be quick and powerful and a discerner of the thoughts
> and intents of the heart . . .[15]

And we who preach today will do well to follow the Puritan lead at this point. Which means that, though the idea for our next sermon may have been triggered by a date (Christmas or Easter, for example), or our hearers' need, felt or unfelt, or our personal experience, perhaps, its clear substance when given must be God's speaking in and through Scripture, via us who preach, who are under the authority of our own message as much as is anybody else. And we must make it crystal clear that what God aims to do is to search us, scour us out, stabilize and strengthen us, and so set us all up for humble, joyful, zealous, eager service of Jesus Christ our Lord.

Conclusion

The thrust of this chapter can be summed up thus: theology helps the preacher as the coach helps the tennis player, grooming and extending his performance by introducing him to the range of strokes that can be made and drilling him in the art of making them correctly. As the coach is the embodiment of decades of experience in playing tennis, so theology is the embodiment of centuries of study, debate and interpretative interaction as the church has sought to understand the Scriptures. One can play tennis after a fashion without ever having been coached, and one can preach from the Bible after a fashion without ever having encountered serious theology in a serious way. But, just as one is likely to play better with coaching, so one is likely to preach better – more perceptively, more searchingly, more fruitfully – when helped by theology; and so the preacher who is theologically competent will, other things being equal, be more use to the church.

Notes

1. 'The exegete who is doing his work properly is forever asking the question: But what is the point? What is the author driving at? That is, he is always raising the question of the author's intent. At the same time, it is to be hoped that he is also asking questions about the content, questions of lexicography, syntax, background, and so forth. And, also, he is wary of overexegeting, for example, finding something that would stagger the author were he informed someone had found it in his writing, or building a theology upon the use of prepositions, or discovering meaning in what was *not* said' (Gordon Fee, 'Hermeneutics and Common Sense', in Roger R. Nicole and J. Ramsey Michaels [eds.], *Inerrancy and Common Sense* [Grand Rapids, Mich.: Baker, 1980], p. 178).

2. For the quadrilateral analysis, see the discussion by Edward Farley, *Theologia: The Fragmentation and Unity of Theological Education* (Philadelphia: Fortress, 1983).

3. Textbooks of systematic theology mostly follow the seven-part order with only minor adjustments; see, for instance, Bruce Milne, *Know the Truth* (Leicester: Inter-Varsity Press, 1982); Millard J. Erickson,

Christian Theology, 3 vols. (Grand Rapids, Mich.: Baker, 1983–5); James
Montgomery Boice, *Foundations of the Christian Faith* (Leicester: Inter-
Varsity Press, 1986); Thomas C. Oden, *Systematic Theology*, 3 vols. (San
Francisco, Calif.: Harper & Row, 1986–92); J.I. Packer, *Concise Theology*
(Wheaton, Ill.: Tyndale, 1993); Wayne Grudem, *Systematic Theology*
(Leicester: Inter-Varsity Press; Grand Rapids, Mich.: Zondervan, 1994);
John M. Frame, *Systematic Theology* (Phillipsburg, N.J.: Presbyterian &
Reformed, 2013); Anthony C. Thiselton, *Systematic Theology* (London:
SPCK; Grand Rapids, Mich.: Eerdmans, 2015).

4. I met it quoted without a reference in Paul King Jewett, *Emil Brunner's
Concept of Revelation* (London: James Clarke, 1954).

5. Ian Breward (ed.), *William Perkins* (Appleford: Sutton Courteney, 1970),
p. 177.

6. This is how Calvin explains the role of his *Institutes*, from the second
edition onward: 'It has *been my purpose . . . to . . .* instruct candidates in
sacred theology for the reading of the divine Word . . . For I believe
I have so embraced the sum of religion in all its parts, and have
arranged it in such an order, that if anyone rightly grasps it, it will not
be difficult for him to determine what he ought especially to seek in
Scripture, and to what end he ought to relate its contents' (*Institutes
of the Christian Religion*, trans. Ford Lewis Battles [Philadelphia:
Westminster, 1967], 1.4).

7. Article 20 of the Church of England's Thirty-Nine Articles.

8. Bible quotations in this chapter are from the New International
Version (1984 ed.) unless otherwise stated.

9. 'The Directory for the Publick Worship of God', in *The Confession
of Faith* (Edinburgh: Banner of Truth, 1985), p. 380.

10. In the 1570s the preaching meetings that Queen Elizabeth I told
Archbishop Grindal to suppress were called prophesyings; and
the first Reformational textbook on preaching in England was *The
Arte of Prophecying*, by William Perkins (*The Workes of that Famous Minister
of Christ in the Universitie of Cambridge, Mr. William Perkins*, 1617, vol. 2,
pp. 646–673; brief extract in Breward, *William Perkins*, pp. 325–349;
full reprint, Edinburgh: Banner of Truth, 1996, 2011).

11. Donald Macleod, 'Preaching and Systematic Theology', in Samuel T.
Logan (ed.), *The Preacher and Preaching* (Phillipsburg, N.J.: Presbyterian
& Reformed, 1986), p. 250.

12. Ibid.

13. The Puritan concept is precisely stated by Jonathan Edwards: '*Affection is* a word that, in its ordinary signification, seems to be something more extensive than *passion*, being used for all vigorous lively actings of the will or inclination . . . As all the exercises of inclination and will are concerned either in approving and liking, or disapproving and rejecting; so the affections are of two sorts; they are those by which the soul is carried out to what is in view, cleaving *to it*, or *seeking it*; or those by which it is averse *from it*, and *opposes it*. Of the former sort are *love, desire, hope, joy, gratitude, complacence*. Of the latter kind are *hatred, fear, anger, grief* and such like . . . And there are some affections wherein there is a *composition* of each of the aforementioned kinds of actings of the will; as in the affection of pity, there is something of the *former kind*, towards the person suffering, and something of the *latter*, towards what he suffers. And so in *zeal*, there is in it high *approbation* of some person or thing, together with vigorous *opposition* to what is conceived to be contrary to it' ('A Treatise Concerning Religious Affections', in H. Hickman [ed.], *The Works of Jonathan Edwards*, vol. 1 [Edinburgh: Banner of Truth, 1974], p. 237).

14. For more discussion of application, see J.I. Packer, 'Method: Speaking for God', in Richard Allen Bodey (ed.), *Inside the Sermon* (Grand Rapids, Mich.: Baker, 1990), pp. 188–190.

15. *Confession of Faith*, p. 380.

3. IS GOD THE ONLY THEOLOGIAN? 'TRUE BUT NOT EXHAUSTIVE'

Michael J. Ovey

Introduction

I first went to university in 1978 to study law and returned to university in 1988 to study theology in preparation for ordination to the presbyterate. In those ten years there had been a sea change. In 1978 so much of the university atmosphere had been strongly empiricist and positivist, with very considerable implicit claims for the powers of human reason and knowledge. The classic question I debated with my fellow law students was whether it was true that Jesus was who he said he was. By 1988 that had changed. The truth question was still there but much more infrequent and in a far more muted form. Instead, there was a pervasive scepticism about any claims to knowledge and there was an unspoken but potent line of argument along these lines:

1. To know something means to know it exhaustively.
2. We do not know God exhaustively.
3. So we do not know God at all.

Arguments along these lines lay behind some of the mantras of the time to the effect that all interpretations of the Bible were equally right and equally wrong; that all a theologian could do was describe the phenomena of religion and not evaluate them for their truth; that a heretic was simply someone with a different perspective from one's own; and so on. These approaches were not new, of course, and writers such as Francis Schaeffer had given us due warning, but these positions were argued with renewed vigour and fervour, not least because of the then chic postmodern imports into the UK's academic life of M. Foucault and J. Derrida, and so on. It all meant that Christian apologists and evangelists working in that university setting had to reconceive their task.

One of the things that made this so painful was the belated recognition that at least part of the postmodern mood was a legitimate reaction against the excessive claims for human rational power that characterized various parts of modernism. To some extent, looking back, I think evangelical Christians had been closer to the rationalists than we should have been and we found it hard to articulate a way of talking about truth without falling over into something like a claim of exhaustive knowledge. Theologically I think our proximity to rationalism was (and perhaps still sometimes is) more toxic than we realized: rationalism is close to the sins of intellectual pride, and pride, argues Augustine, is fundamental to human sin.[1] Claims to exhaustive knowledge have an ugly way of blurring the distinction between creature and creator in the realm of knowledge. To this extent the postmodern rebuke was more apt than we might care to admit.

But what response should there be to it? There are many reasons for being thankful for the ministry of Don Carson, but an extremely significant one is the work he did in the late 1980s and early 1990s in explaining and popularizing the notion that Christians can genuinely know the truth without falling into the hubris of claiming an exhaustive knowledge of truth. We know truly but not exhaustively.

The ramifications of this elegant formula were far-reaching. It encouraged us to invite people to consider Christ and his claims in terms of their truth. It gave vitality to discipling people in terms of knowing God. It helped provide a framework within which one could challenge heterodox theologies without being immediately ruled out of court because one was 'really a rationalist'.

In what follows I want to explore and flesh out this idea of knowing truly but not exhaustively in the light of a distinction employed by Reformed and some Lutheran theologians in the sixteenth and seventeenth centuries, namely the distinction between archetypal and ectypal theologies and their relationship. I shall argue that this distinction helps us to be genuine theologians, speaking as creatures truly yet humbly of God to his glory and magnifying his grace.

Archetypal and Ectypal Theology

Protestant scholastics – with whom the archetypal–ectypal distinction is strongly associated – have an unenviable reputation in some circles.[2] In particular the fear is that such theology separates God as creator off from God as redeemer and has an implicitly rationalist bent.[3] On this view, using a Protestant Scholastic distinction seems fraught with danger because it may open the door to just the kind of rationalistic arrogance against which the postmodern mood rightly reacts.

This line of criticism suggests that there is something deeply flawed in the very way that some Protestant scholastics conceive of the theological project, a flaw, so to speak, before one even starts, a mistake at the level of theological prolegomena. In fact, this chapter will argue that the theological prolegomenon of the archetypal–ectypal distinction resists rationalism and integrates the doctrines of God as creator and redeemer. In what follows, our primary dialogue partner will be Franciscus Junius, with some comparative material from Polanus, who closely mirrors him on this question.

Junius sets out his argument in thirty-nine theses in his *A Treatise on True Theology*.[4] We join his argument at thesis three: 'Thesis three: Even if all believe that theology exists, nevertheless it is commonly spoken of in two ways. For one theology is true, the other is false and subject to opinion.'[5]

Naturally, this immediately puts Junius and those following him at odds with some contemporary approaches. Not all 'theologies' are true. And by putting this distinction so early in his argument Junius indicates that this difference is fundamental. It has a biblical resonance because of the way that the Bible draws a fundamental distinction between true worship of God and idolatry, a distinction in which idolatry is associated with lie and not truth (Isa. 44:20 is a classic example of the lie connotation). In this way Junius takes us well beyond a 'religious studies' approach, which seeks only to describe a religious belief system or to treat it phenomenologically. A key question is whether that belief system is true.

Moreover, it is a question of the truth about God and of the truth of things in relation to him. Thus 'theology' is theocentric, as Junius proceeds: 'Thesis five: Theology is wisdom concerning divine matters.'[6]

It is at this point that Junius goes on to distinguish archetypal from ectypal theology: 'Thesis six: This theology is either archetypal, undoubtedly the wisdom of God himself, or it is ectypal, having been fashioned by God.'[7]

This way of putting things is highly representative of later Protestant scholastics. Thus the English writer Edward Leigh puts his summary distinction like this:

> Theology or *Divinity* is two-fold, either first, Archetypal, or *Divinity* in God, of God himself, by which God by one individual and immutable act knows himself in himself, and all other things out of himself, by himself. Or second, Ectypal and communicated, expressed in us by Divine Revelation after the Patern [*sic*] and Idea which is in God, and this is called *Theologia de Deo*, Divinity concerning God, which is after to be defined.[8]

We need now to draw this basic distinction out in more detail.

Archetypal theology

Basically, archetypal theology is God's theology. It is both reflexive (God's knowledge of himself) and of all other things. It is intimately connected with and arises from God's unique knowledge and way of knowing. The connection with God's knowledge is evident, as Junius explains:

> [Archetypal] theology is the very same thing as unbounded wisdom, which God possesses concerning his own person and all other things, as they have been set in order with respect to him necessarily, individually,

and by an uninterrupted relation among themselves. This happens according to his own infinite reason.[9]

And once the connection with God's knowing or wisdom is established, one has to think about the uniqueness of God's way of knowing. Leigh catches it well with his phrase that God 'by one individual and immutable act knows himself in himself, and all other things out of himself, by himself'.[10] The language of knowing as one individual immutable act is very much the terminology of God's omniscience. Thus when commenting on God's omniscience, Leigh writes:

> For the manner of Divine Knowledge, God knows all things by his Essence, not by Species abstracted from the things; for so things should be before the Divine Knowledge, on which yet they depend. God doth not understand by discoursing from a known thing to that which is unknown, in a doubtful and successive reasoning; but by looking on them, and by one most simple individual and eternal Act comprehending all things.[11]

Thus Junius can produce the following thesis: 'Thesis seven: Archetypal theology is the divine wisdom of divine matters. Indeed, we stand in awe before this and do not seek to trace it out.'[12]

Several things stand out. First, while this theology deals, like all true theology with divine matters, this is *divine* wisdom. It is God's alone. It is unique to God because of the uniqueness of God. Two aspects of God's uniqueness in particular underlie this: first, that God is uncreated and second, that God is the creator of all things by his will from nothing.

With regard to his uncreatedness, the triune God alone is uncreated and therefore able to know himself immediately and perfectly. By definition in the case of a creature there is something that created one, and one does not know the circumstances prior to one's own creation. A creature necessarily has limited direct self-knowledge.

With regard to being creator, since God creates all things and upholds their existence by his will, all things are known to him, both individually and also in their relation to each other and in relation to himself. By virtue of this, God could satisfy the old, elusive criterion of 'knowledge' to the effect that true knowledge is 'true justified belief'. One issue of that criterion has been that genuine 'justification' requires the ability to know an object of knowledge in its relation to all other objects everywhere. Put bluntly, one has to know everything in order to know anything. Of course, to God, as uncreated creator of all, such knowledge is not a chimaera.

It is for this reason that Polanus can say, 'Theology in its most proper sense is that knowledge which is in the divine mind about divine matters. In that way God alone is said to be a theologian; and further God is understood to be the first, best and most perfect theologian.'[13]

To this extent archetypal theology is necessarily perfect because the perfections of God include a knowledge that does not depend on accruing knowledge and understanding of observed phenomena or by reading accounts of those who have themselves grown in understanding in these ways. Junius and others stress that this knowledge is without growth and succession in the mind of God. He knows all things by one immediate act, not by a cumulative process of discursive reasoning. God knows truly and exhaustively. In fact, one might say he is able to know as truly as he does precisely because he does know exhaustively. God's wisdom 'comprehends the whole at the same time and wholly'.[14]

This perfection carries a necessary corollary: it is beyond question and disagreement. As Junius writes, '[W]e stand in awe before this and do not seek to trace it out'.[15] If it is perfect and true, then dissent from it must necessarily be imperfect and untrue.

However, the next issue relates precisely to the uniqueness of archetypal theology. God's archetypal theology is unique because he is the unique, uncreated creator of all from nothing. This certainly upholds the creator–creature distinction robustly. But it is just there that more questions arise. It is all very well for Polanus to point out the perfection of God's theology, but how does this help human theology? Junius and others point out that such archetypal theology is incommunicable. After all, being uncreated – an essential basis in God's self-knowledge – cannot be shared with a creature.[16] The creature would not be a creature if it had that kind of self-knowledge.

At this point one might ask if the net effect of this line of argument is to leave human theology in the position one sometimes associates with Kant: that God is separate from us and we can know nothing about him. It is true that there are different reasons in play. For Kant this is because knowledge is ultimately associated with the perception of things in the world, and since God is not in the world he cannot be known in that way. For the Protestant scholastics God's knowledge is related to his perfection and infinity, to which we do not have access. But is the net result not the same? And so all the problems of talking about one particular human theology or family of theologies as 'true' remains problematic to the point of impossibility.

This naturally takes us to a consideration of the other kind of theology that is 'true'. Before we do this, though, it is worth noting a nuance to the language of incommunicability. By saying archetypal knowledge is incommunicable, we are saying that the mode of knowing, that of being the uncreated creator of all things from nothing, cannot be shared. Put sharply, it is saying that we cannot know as God knows. Naturally, this leaves open the possibility of knowing but not as God knows. We turn now to the way in which the Protestant scholastics thought that was possible: ectypal theology.

Ectypal theology

After discussing archetypal theology, Junius goes on to the other kind of true theology. He introduces it like this: '[T]he second theology [ectypal theology] is that wisdom which the creatures have concerning God according to their own manner, and concerning those things that are oriented towards God through his communication of himself'.[17] He later puts this in thesis form as follows: 'Thesis eight: Ectypal theology, whether taken in itself, as they say, or relatively in relation to something else, is the wisdom of divine matters, fashioned by God from the archetype of himself, through the communication of grace for his own glory.'[18]

Several things stand out from these two statements. First the subject matter is the same as theology more generally: divine matters.

Secondly, this theology is genuinely human in two important senses. To begin with, this is the wisdom about divine matters that humans have ('which the creatures have concerning God').[19] But further it is a wisdom that is held as creatures or in, one might say, a creaturely way ('according to their own manner').[20] This matters because it upholds the integrity of the distinction between creature and creator. Ectypal theology is not a subtle way of blurring that distinction so that human theologians know 'as if' we were God.

Thirdly, this wisdom originates in God and in his archetypal theological knowledge. It is not humanly originated, although it is humanly held. Junius writes of an ectypal theology that is 'fashioned by God from the archetype of himself',[21] and of 'his communication of himself'.[22] Leigh in similar terms observes that ectypal theology 'is communicated, expressed in us by Divine Revelation after the Patern [sic] and Idea which is in God'.[23]

This means that the Protestant scholastics are drawing a distinction between 'incommunicable', understood as a sharing of one thing with another person, where one holds or has it in precisely the same way as that other; and 'communicated', where a genuine sharing has taken place, where two persons hold an idea or affect but not in the same way. The Protestant scholastics are certainly asserting archetypal theology is incommunicable in that first sense but that this does not prevent its being communicated in the second sense. In a similar vein, when I am at a wedding and hear the groom declare his love for his bride, his affect is in an important sense incommunicable. I do not feel his love for his bride as he feels it (in fact, it is important that I do not). On the other hand, while he cannot in that full sense communicate his love to me and the other members of the congregation, he can communicate to the rest of us that he loves the woman facing him. The fact that I cannot share his love in the sense of loving her as he loves does not preclude me knowing that he loves and that his love is directed towards a particular person, his bride.

Thus the connection that is being asserted between archetypal and ectypal theology is that archetypal theology is the source of ectypal theology, but remains different from it, and that the connection is one established by God, the one who has archetypal theology. This is vital: only the one with archetypal theological knowledge could validate a theology that derives from archetypal theology. The connection lies on the Godward side of the creator–creature divide, not on the creature's side. Junius underlines this: '[F]or God himself alone, not however any created thing, is the efficient cause of that disposition which we call theology'.[24]

This means that ectypal theology has a dual aspect: it is creaturely in that creatures may hold it according to their natures as creatures but it is emphatically not creaturely in the sense that it is devised by creatures. It is in fact created itself in that God originates it. As a created thing it is not the same as archetypal theology which is as perfect and uncreated as the God who 'holds' it. Junius expands on the relationship yet difference between archetypal and ectypal theology:

> [B]ut the attributes of this theology [ectypal theology] are very different from those which we assigned previously to that archetypal theology. For this one is created, it is dispositional nor is it absolute except in its own mode but rather finite, discreet, and divinely communicated it is, as it were, a true and definite image of that theology which we have explained is uncreated, essential or formal, most absolute, infinite, at once complete, and incommunicable. It is created, for it is not of the creator in himself, but it is from the creator in the subject which he himself created.[25]

Put this way, ectypal theology is God's created gift of knowledge of divine matters to his human creatures in terms conformed by him to their creatureliness. His gift is patterned on his own archetypal knowledge but is adapted to the finitude (and fallenness) of his human creatures. Both Polanus and Junius stress the association with grace and glory. God communicates his grace graciously by the gift of ectypal theology and this aims at the glorification of God. It is hard here to miss the biblical associations of Ephesians 1:3 ff. with the refrain that God has done the saving deeds that he has to the praise of his glorious grace.

Returning briefly to one of the criticisms of Protestant scholasticism, creation and redemption are brought together here because the grace of redemption is known in ectypal theology by the grace of the uncreated creator of all in communicating in ways proportioned to the creature his own knowledge of himself and what he has done.

Within this basic account of ectypal theology, the convention for Protestant scholastics was to distinguish three types of ectypal theology: a theology of *union* (the theology that Jesus Christ possessed by virtue of the integrity of his human nature); a theology of *vision* (possessed by redeemed humanity in the fulfilment of the ages); and a theology of *revelation*.[26]

The theology of revelation itself divides into natural and supernatural. Turretin summarizes like this:

> The natural, occupied with that which may be known of God (*to gnōston tou Theou*), is both innate (from the common notions implanted in each one) and acquired (which creatures gain discursively). This was exquisite in Adam before his fall, but is highly disordered in corrupted man. The supernatural (which transcends our reason and is communicated to us by God by the new light of grace so that we may obtain the enjoyment of the highest good, which was revealed to the patriarchs before as well as after the flood, and through Moses delivered by God to the people of Israel, and is called the Old Testament or the New Testament, which is called by way of eminence 'Christian' because it has Christ for its author and object) is from Christ (Jn. 1:18) and speaks of him (Acts 1:1; 1 Cor 2:2). It is strictly called 'revealed' because its first principle is divine revelation strictly taken and made through the word, not through creatures.[27]

The net effect of this is that the ectypal theology of revelation is now focused on the supernatural revelation. Turretin emphasizes that natural revelation is distorted by the Fall and critically does not provide saving knowledge of God as Redeemer.[28] To this extent, the category of ectypal natural revelation does not open the door to a rationalistic theological enterprise. Instead, Turretin emphasizes again the origin of supernatural revealed ectypal theology ('communicated to us by God'[29]), which precludes the idea that it is 'creaturely' in the sense of being solely originated by creatures. This in turn leaves space for a revelation that 'transcends our reason'.[30]

It is important to develop this latter point a little. One of the problems of human reason in any theology is the way it can act as a limiter on what we may know about God. Starkly, we may refuse to entertain a theological proposal because our reason rules it out of court. Thus Hilary of Poitiers famously reflected on the Arian controversy that with both Arians and Sabellians the orthodox were dealing with those who confined what could be to what they could rationally conceive.[31] The difficulty of course, is that any infinite God will not be comprehensible to a finite human creature. His uncreated infinity is not in that sense communicable to his finite creatures. Hence our need to rely on his witness to himself, his revelation, as Hilary repeatedly insists.

Thus it is significant that Turretin states, first, that revelation transcends human reason,[32] and secondly that reason has only a 'ministerial', 'servant' or 'auxiliary' use in proper theology. Turretin explains:

> A ministerial and organic relation is quite different from a principal and despotic. Reason holds the former relation to theology, not the latter. It is the Hagar (the bondmaid which should be in subjection to Scripture); not the Sarah (the mistress which presides over Scripture). It ought to compare the things proposed to be believed with the sacred Scriptures, the inflexible rule of truth. As when we refer the things we wish to measure to the public standard with the hand and eye. But reason itself neither can nor ought to be constituted the rule of belief.[33]

It is in this vein that Junius can comment on the ectypal revealed theology of the Bible:

> [O]ur theology is the wisdom of divine matters, communicated by revelation through the spirit of God by the kindness of his nature of grace with those who dwell on earth; according to which theology they contemplate God and his divine matters by intellectual light, though by a transient and incomplete reason, through their own advances, until they attain a perfect vision of him on to his glory.[34]

Implications

This means that the archetypal–ectypal distinction provides a way of speaking about a theology held by creatures in a creaturely way, but which transcends creaturely limitations at least in part in speaking of the creator because the creator himself originates or creates this theology, in particular the ectypal revelational theology of the Bible. The creator can adapt his 'created' ectypal theology to his human creatures precisely because he is the creator of both. In all this, he is shown as gracious because the content of what he reveals (salvation in Christ) is gracious and the mode is gracious too: he condescends to express truths about his infinite perfection in terms adapted to finite human creatures.

Several things follow from this. First, one must be clear that there is a distinction between creator and creature; if one blurs that distinction then the distinction between archetypal and ectypal theology will also be blurred. This blurring is a potent temptation to pride. Secondly, this suggests a unity in the way the Bible should be read. If the Bible is the ectypal expression of God's archetypal theology and that archetypal theology is rooted in the unique, unified perfection of the one true God, then the old Reformation principle that one must read scripture with scripture first of all is well founded. It is the practical outworking of the way ectypal theology is grounded in archetypal theology. This in turn means that as one reads different books with different styles from different periods from different authors this diversity should not be allowed to override the admittedly complex unity that ectypal theology has by virtue of its character as originating in the gift of the one true God.

The character of ectypal theology as gift also profoundly shapes our responses to it. As a gift of God it should be received with thankfulness and without a sense of ownership. H. Thielicke perceptively comments on the passion of the possessor that can creep over a theologian, and a healthy recognition that ectypal theology originates in God reminds us that the Bible is not a wax nose for us to mould as we please. Such an attitude would speak of us thinking ourselves possessors or consumers of ectypal revelation rather than as those who receive it as a created instrument of God's blessing for his human creatures. In fact, the theologian who handles ectypal theological revelation as if its meaning originated in him or her runs a significant risk of acting as though ectypal theology were that human's own creation or a creation of a human community. Certainly we need to account for the human dimension of the authorship of the biblical books, but equally clearly this must not be used to minimize or diminish the significance of divine authorship.

This opens up an uncomfortable avenue of enquiry for theologians. The trajectory of the Protestant scholastic argument is that ectypal revelational theology is a created gift communicating God's grace to us, primarily for his glory and secondarily for our salvific benefit. The inevitable questions we find it hard to ask of our various theologies, which are meant to arise from this ectypal theology, are threefold:

- Does my theology acknowledge that proper theology in its truthfulness about divine matters ultimately arises as a gift of God, not from my intellectual merit? It is perilously easy to think that salvation is by grace but we do theology by meritorious works.
- Does my theology celebrate God for his undeserved kindness?
- Does my theology glorify him first or rather me as the great discoverer or solver of his riddles?

Much of this traces back, in Reinhold Niebuhr's terms, to our race's pride of knowledge, and that in turn Niebuhr traces back to our disaffection for being creatures of God rather than his peers or even his superiors. Niebuhr writes, 'Man [sic] is ignorant and involved in the limitations of a finite mind; but he pretends that he is not limited. He assumes that he can gradually transcend finite limitations until his mind becomes identical with universal mind.'[35]

But this is the great thing about Don Caron's simple dictum: we can speak of God truly but not exhaustively; truly, because the creator brings forth an ectypal theology; but not exhaustively, because the creator has given us as his creatures ectypal theology, but not archetypal theology. For all the intellectual challenges 'theology' brings, there is also the personal challenge: does one do it as the humble human creature of this uncreated and redeeming God? Or as someone who sees no need to recognize one's identity as created?

Notes

1. On pride generally and the pride of knowledge in particular, see Reinhold Niebuhr, *The Nature and Destiny of Man* (London: Nisbet, 1941), pp. 200ff. For Augustine on pride, see (e.g.) *City of God* 14.28 and 12.6, where he remarks, 'The beginning of all sin is pride.'

2. See the helpful summary in W.J. van Asselt, 'The Fundamental Meaning of Theology: Archetypal and Ectypal Theology in Seventeenth-Century Reformed Thought', *Westminster Theological Journal* 64 (2002), pp. 319–335 (at pp. 319–320).

3. Ibid., pp. 319–320.

4. A very helpful English translation by D.C. Noe is available (Grand Rapids, Mich.: Reformation Heritage, 2014).

5. Junius, *A Treatise on True Theology*, ch. 1.

6. Ibid., ch. 2.

7. Ibid., ch. 3.

8. Edward Leigh, *A Systeme or Body of Divinity* (London: A.M. for William Lee, 1654), 1.1 (p. 2).

9. Junius, *Treatise*, ch. 3.

10. Leigh, *Systeme*, 1.1 (p. 2).

11. Ibid. 2.7 (p. 160).

12. Junius, *Treatise*, ch. 4.

13. Polanus, *Syntagma*, lib I cap iii ('Theologia ergo propriissime est illa notitia, quae est in mente divina de rebus divinis. Isto modo solus Deus dicitur Theologus; ac proinde Deus intelligitur esse primus, optimus et perfectissimus Theologus').

14. Junius, *Treatise*, ch. 4.

15. Ibid.

16. Ibid.

17. Ibid., ch. 3.

18. Ibid., ch. 5.

19. Ibid., ch. 3.

20. Ibid.

21. Ibid., ch. 5.

22. Ibid., ch. 3.

23. Leigh, *Systeme*, 1.1 (p. 2).

24. Junius, *Treatise*, ch. 5.

25. Ibid.

26. See (e.g.) F. Turretin, *Institutes of Elenctic Theology*, Topic I. Q 2. VI.

27. Ibid., Q 2. VII.

28. Ibid., Q 4. V and VI.

29. Ibid., Q 2. VII.

30. Ibid.

31. Hilary of Poitiers, *De Trinitate* 1.15.

32. Turretin, *Institutes*, Topic I. Q 2. VII.

33. Ibid., Q 8. VI.

34. Junius, *Treatise*, ch. 8.

35. Niebuhr, *Nature and Destiny*, vol. 1, p. 190.

Part II

4. THE PRIORITY OF TRUTH – JESUS AND PAUL ON REASON AND TRUTH

Stefan Gustavsson

Recently I heard someone saying, 'People generally cannot believe themselves so easily manipulated and controllable. This is precisely why they are so easy to manipulate and control.' The apostle Paul was well aware of the danger of manipulation. In 2 Corinthians he tells us that he and his colleagues deliberately 'renounced secret and shameful ways; we do not use deception, nor do we distort the word of God. On the contrary, by setting forth the truth plainly we commend ourselves to everyone's conscience in the sight of God' (4:2).[1]

This attitude is seen in many places in Paul's ministry. The book of Acts (17:10–12) says that when he and Silas arrived in Berea

> they went to the Jewish synagogue. Now the Berean Jews were of more noble character than those in Thessalonica, for they received the message with great eagerness and examined the Scriptures every day to see if what Paul said was true. As a result, many of them believed, as did also a number of prominent Greek women and many Greek men.

It is obvious that Paul put a great deal of trust in *the truth* of the message he proclaimed. Its validity was not dependent on his

authority as a leader or his rhetorical skills. He willingly gave people
the freedom to scrutinize the veracity of his claims. The Jews at the
synagogue therefore decided to reread their own scriptures to check
whether it was true that Jesus is the promised Messiah: '[They]
examined the Scriptures every day to see if what Paul said was true.'
And they realized that what Paul said was correct: 'As a result, many
of them believed.'

For Paul the gospel clearly belongs to the category of truth. He
would have no problem with the famous definition of truth that we
have from Aristotle, that truth means correspondence to reality: 'To
say of what is that it is not, or of what is not that it is, is false, while
to say of what is that it is, and of what is not that it is not, is true;
so that he who says of anything that it is, or that it is not, will say
either what is true or what is false.'[2]

The gospel is grounded in the God who is really there. He is not
a God far away and unknown. According to Paul, 'he has not left
himself without testimony'. His fingerprints mark the world around
us; he is the one who even 'fills your hearts with joy' (Acts 14:17).
More than that, the gospel is grounded in real historical events: it is
about a historical person, Jesus of Nazareth, his life, death and
resurrection. It does not belong to the category of fantasy or faith.
That is why Paul, after presenting the good news about Jesus Christ,
can challenge both the Roman procurator Festus and the Jewish
king Agrippa: 'What I am saying is true and reasonable. The king is
familiar with these things, and I can speak freely to him. I am
convinced that none of this has escaped his notice, because it was
not done in a corner' (Acts 26:25–26).

Jesus – in Dialogue and Debate

Paul's attitude to his message is in fact just a reflection of what we
see in the life of Jesus.

What characterized Jesus during his three years in the public eye?
For most Christians, three particular things spring to mind immediately. First, Jesus was a *preacher*. He proclaimed his message in
the synagogues and gave immortal sermons, such as the Sermon
on the Mount. Secondly, Jesus was a *miracle maker*. He healed the sick
and the possessed and fed thousands of people in a supernatural

way. Even the dead were brought back to life. Thirdly, Jesus was *love incarnate*. He saw the outcasts, touched the lepers, associated freely with people on the fringes of society, with suspect women and corrupt men. He manifested the essence of love through his life.

All of this is true. But I wish to add a fourth dimension, namely, *Jesus as an apologist* arguing for the truth of his message.

A review of the four Gospels shows how strikingly often Jesus took part in dialogues and debates. To a large extent, the Gospel texts are one long, ongoing conversation that Jesus conducted with different people. This claim can easily be corroborated with the help of statistics. If you search for the terms *asked* and *answered* in the four Gospels using a modern Bible program, you will get the following results for the NIV 2011: 'asked' 303 times, 'answered' 144 times. Discourse and dialogue were evidently central to Jesus.

In dialogues, Jesus often challenged his audience to use their common sense, to think matters through, to question their own prejudice and hasty claims, to analyse their own positions and draw the right conclusions. This part of Jesus' teaching – *how he challenged his listeners to think independently and critically* – is often overlooked. As Jesus says, 'Stop judging by mere appearances, but instead judge correctly' (John 7:24). In other words: do not make superficial, prejudiced judgements. Make correct assessments. Jesus made similar appeals on a number of occasions in the Gospels:

- 'Do you still not understand?' (Matt. 16:9)
- 'What do you think?' (Matt. 18:12)
- 'What do you think?' (Matt. 21:28)
- 'Are you so dull?' (Mark 7:18)
- 'Why don't you judge for yourselves what is right?' (Luke 12:57)
- 'Why is my language not clear to you?' (John 8:43)

When asked which commandment in the Law was the greatest, Jesus replied by combining two passages from the Scriptures, Deuteronomy 6 and Leviticus 19:

> One of the teachers of the law came and heard them debating. Noticing that Jesus had given them a good answer, he asked him, 'Of all the commandments, which is the most important?'

'The most important one,' answered Jesus, 'is this: "Hear, O Israel: The Lord our God, the Lord is one. Love the Lord your God with all your heart and with all your soul and with all your mind and with all your strength." The second is this: "Love your neighbour as yourself." There is no commandment greater than these.' (Mark 12:28–31)

It is interesting to note that in formal terms, Jesus did not quote the source correctly. If you look up Deuteronomy 6:5, you discover that the passage speaks of loving the Lord your God 'with all your heart and with all your soul and with all your strength'. There is nothing about the mind! What Jesus does is to provide a *clarification*: We should not leave out our mind!

The point of the Old Testament passage is that human beings are called to love God with our whole being, with our hearts, our souls and our strength. That is, we are to love him with everything that we are and have. From the Hebrew perspective *the heart* is not merely a symbol of our emotions; it is the centre of the whole personality and encompasses reason as well.

We can further note that each time Deuteronomy 6 is quoted in other passages in the Gospels it is quoted with varying degrees of detail but each time *reason is appended to the original*:

- Luke: heart, soul, strength, mind (10:27)
- Matthew: heart, soul, mind (strength is not mentioned) (22:37)
- Mark: heart, understanding [mind], strength (soul is not mentioned) (12:33)

Given that humankind has been created in God's image, the requirement for us to use reason is self-evident. The entire outlook of the Bible is that God speaks to humankind and uses human language to do so, which requires reason to understand. Consider God's instructions to humankind at creation (Gen. 1 – 2):

- Be fruitful and increase in number (1:28)
- Fill the earth and subdue it (1:28)
- Work the garden and take care of it (2:15)
- Name the animals (2:19)

These instructions presuppose that God wants humankind to use rationality fully to love and honour their Maker. That is exactly what Jesus emphasizes in his teachings.

Jesus and Children

Several passages in the New Testament stress that a Christian should not be like a child. In 1 Corinthians 14:20 Paul writes, 'Brothers and sisters, stop thinking like children. In regard to evil be infants, but in your thinking be adults.' We come across the same train of thought in Ephesians 4:14: 'Then we will no longer be infants, tossed back and forth by the waves, and blown here and there by every wind of teaching and by the cunning and craftiness of people in their deceitful scheming.'

Thus *naïveté*, ignorance and childishness are not Christian virtues. But how does this relate to Jesus' positive invitation that we *should* become like children? Is Paul on a collision course with his Master on this subject?

We need to take into account that both children and adults may have negative traits from which we want to distance ourselves as well as positive traits that we want to highlight. Thus Jesus uses children as a *warning example* when he criticizes religious leaders. In Matthew 11:16–17 he says, 'To what can I compare this generation? They are like children sitting in the market-places and calling out to others: "We played the pipe for you, and you did not dance; we sang a dirge, and you did not mourn."' Childishness and immaturity are not Christian virtues.

In other passages, however, children are put forward by Jesus as *models to emulate*: '[U]nless you change and become like little children, you will never enter the kingdom of heaven', he says (Matt. 18:3). But what is it about the children that he highlights? The key is provided in the subsequent verse: 'Therefore, whoever takes the lowly position of this child is the greatest in the kingdom of heaven' (Matt. 18:4). It is a child's *humility*, not his or her lack of knowledge or immature reason, that Jesus emphasizes.

The point is not that each child is always humble, for who has not encountered obstinate and self-focused children, or been one himself? Jesus was well aware of that. No, his point is the humility displayed by children who accept their position *as children*, as they allow themselves to be carried and hugged by their parents and recognize their fundamental dependence. Children are aware that they cannot claim full autonomy vis-à-vis their parents.

Jesus and Paul are in agreement. We should be 'adults in our thinking' and we should 'love God with all our mind'. And that of course precludes all manipulation.

Athens and the Foolishness of the Cross

But is Paul really coherent in his thinking about truth and about the place of arguments and reason? There is a myth about Paul and the two cities of Athens and Corinth, arising from a book published in 1892 by New Testament scholar William Ramsay, who claimed that Paul considered his apologetic speech in Athens to be a failure. Paul was 'disappointed and perhaps disillusioned by his experience in Athens. He felt that he had gone at least as far as was right in the way of presenting his doctrine in a form suited to the current philosophy; and the result had been little more than nothing.'[3]

From Athens, Paul continued on to Corinth, where, according to Ramsay, he decided to abandon the approach he had tried in Athens. That is Ramsay's interpretation of 1 Corinthians 2:2: 'For I resolved to know nothing while I was with you except Jesus Christ and him crucified.' Ramsay suggests that Paul dissociated himself from apologetics and arguments and henceforth focused exclusively on proclaiming the death and resurrection of Jesus, no longer bothering to explain, defend, reason or argue.

Unfortunately this idea did not die along with Ramsay. It gained a life of its own and is passed on in many contexts without being examined closely. Too many Bible readers, without knowing about Ramsay, have embraced the theory about Paul's 'change of heart' between Athens and Corinth. But is this idea correct?

A person reading 1 Corinthians 1 – 2 can easily get the impression that Paul does in fact distance himself from reason and reflection, from using arguments and apologetics, and advocates only the proclamation of Jesus' death and resurrection. Paul does write critically about 'wisdom', and speaks of the 'foolishness of

God' and the 'foolishness of the cross', as if the gospel is something unreasonable, to be believed despite all that contradicts it. Is that what Paul meant? How should we evaluate what happened in Athens and how should we understand 1 Corinthians?

Let us begin with the *assessment of Paul's speech in Athens*. There are a number of convincing arguments that Ramsay's theory is completely wrong and should be put to rest. Let us look at three of them:

First, *Luke does not even hint that the speech in Athens was a failure.* On the contrary, he highlights the speech before the Areopagus, allowing it to take up considerable space in his text, as if it were a model speech.

Secondly, *the results in Athens were encouraging.* In order to make a correct assessment we must not compare apples and oranges. Peter's speech in Jerusalem at Pentecost, when thousands came to faith, cannot be our basis for comparison. The event at Pentecost was unique. Neither is it reasonable to compare Athens with the various occasions when Paul spoke in synagogues when 'many' came to believe. For the listeners in the synagogues, the step to accepting the gospel was smaller than it was for the Gentiles in Athens: Jews already believed in the God of Israel, in the message of the Scriptures and the promise of a future Messiah. What did transpire in Athens? A number of people came to faith following Paul's speech: even Dionysius, who was a member of the Areopagus, and Damaris, most likely a distinguished woman as she is mentioned together with Dionysius. A number of other people also believed. That can hardly be called a failure.

Thirdly, *Paul did not alter his strategy after Athens.* His work in Corinth is described as 'trying to persuade Jews and Greeks' (Acts 18:4), and his enemies accuse him of 'persuading the people' (Acts 18:13). He continued to reason in order to convince. As can be seen in the book of Acts from chapters 9 to 28, Paul consistently used apologetics. Nothing changed after Athens.

Wisdom and Foolishness in Corinth

So what did Paul mean in 1 Corinthians 1 – 2? To understand correctly what he meant we need to be aware of background facts. After all, 'Context is King'.

An example of how critical context is to correct interpretation is evident in contemporary global politics. Many journalists have observed that Russian President Putin's physical movements are peculiar. His walk and the way he swings his arms led many to guess that he had contracted Parkinson's disease or some other illness. The truth turned out to be entirely different. A study published by *The BMJ* (*British Medical Journal*) notes that Putin has shown a 'clearly reduced right-sided arm swing', possibly related to weapons training he received when he was part of the Soviet KGB. 'KGB operatives were instructed to keep their weapon in their right hand close to their chest and to move forward with one side, usually the left, presumably allowing subjects to draw the gun as quickly as possible when confronted with a foe.'[4] The theory is that Putin may have so trained himself in this way of moving that it has become natural to him. It is as though he is saying, 'Look, I have had KGB training, I am a real man,' explains Bastiaan Bloem, professor of movement disorder neurology in the Netherlands.[5]

The interpretation that was natural to us, that Putin is unwell and therefore enfeebled, was incorrect. To someone with the right background knowledge, Putin's walk and his stiff right arm held close to the body signal strength, the opposite of weakness.

What then is the correct context for Paul's letter to the community in Corinth? First, *Paul's situation when he wrote 1 Corinthians.* Paul states in the epistle that he is in Ephesus: 'But I will stay on at Ephesus until Pentecost' (16:8). We know from the reference to the proconsul Gallio (Acts 18:12) that Paul left Corinth early in the sixth decade of the first century and travelled to Ephesus, where he stayed for two years. That is where he wrote 1 Corinthians in the year 53 or 54. From the book of Acts we also know *how* he worked in Ephesus during the time that he wrote to the community in Corinth:

> Paul entered the synagogue and spoke boldly there for three
> months, *arguing persuasively about the kingdom of God.* But some of
> them became obstinate; they refused to believe and publicly maligned
> the Way. So Paul left them. He took the disciples with him and had
> discussions daily in the lecture hall of Tyrannus. (Acts 19:8–9, italics
> added)

It is inconceivable that Paul would have used all his energy to argue for the kingdom of God in Ephesus, while simultaneously writing to Corinth that the message he was proclaiming was foolish and impossible to defend through arguments.

Secondly, *the situation of the Christians in Corinth*. The city of Corinth was a young, dynamic city, a cultural melting pot under many influences. Dio Chrysostom was a contemporary philosopher and historian. Describing a visit to Corinth in a letter, he commented on the confusion that prevailed in the entire region during the Isthmian Games, the second largest event after the Olympic Games:

> crowds of wretched sophists around Poseidon's temple shouting and reviling one another, and their disciples . . . fighting with one another, many writers reading aloud their stupid works, many poets reciting the poems while others applauded them, many jugglers showing their tricks, many fortunetellers interpreting fortunes, lawyers innumerable perverting judgment and peddlers not a few peddling whatever they happened to have.[6]

The 'wretched sophists' were itinerant philosophy teachers and experts in rhetoric. We know that many of them were sceptics. They believed that there is no objective truth or morals. They concluded that they were free to act in a manner that benefited themselves, and that rhetoric could help them achieve that. The objective of rhetoric was to convince those in power that what was in the speaker's interest was what was best for the rulers. To achieve this the orator had to learn to defend any assertion. The most skilful speaker was the one able to defend the least believable position.

This approach was criticized during classical antiquity. The philosopher Philostratus called it 'theatrical shamelessness' and described it as 'flowery, bombastic, full of startling metaphors, too metrical, too dependent on tricks of rhetoric, too emotional'.[7] Others made comparisons with the medical profession, saying that that sort of rhetoric was like a physician who brought flowers and perfume instead of medicine.[8] Plutarch described it as 'swashbuckling and boastful, full of empty exultation'.[9]

Image and appearance were of great importance to the itinerant rhetoricians of classical antiquity. They set up what we today would call performances, during which they charmed their audiences. According to Dio Chrysostom, the orators were mostly concerned about their reputations and never said things to hurt or offend their listeners; they presented and embellished that which the audience already held to be true. This was done for payment, and, as we know, in the marketplace the customer is always right.[10]

With this background knowledge much in 1 Corinthians becomes clearer. Paul is not opposing reason and arguments; he is opposing a certain type of rhetoric. He has not come to impress or get the admiration of the listeners. He does not trumpet his message for payment. Paul refused to adapt to the corrupt rhetorical tradition of Corinth and was apparently criticized for failing to do so. He quotes the Corinthians in 2 Corinthians 10:10: 'For some say, "His letters are weighty and forceful, but in person he is unimpressive and his speaking amounts to nothing."'

As New Testament scholar Ben Witherington explains:

> Not persuasion, not rhetoric in general, but sophistry – the use of words 'full of sound and fury, but signifying nothing' is what Paul is eschewing here. There is of course a difference between the rhetoric of mere display, or eloquence for its own sake (pure sophistry), and substantive rhetoric.[11]

What Paul objects to in 1 Corinthians is *the manipulative rhetoric of the sophists*, not the use of reason or arguments. That is why he chose the term 'eloquence' at the beginning and end of 1:17 – 2:1, in which the wisdom of the world is contrasted with the wisdom of God:

- 'For Christ did not send me to baptize, but to preach the gospel – not with wisdom and *eloquence*, lest the cross of Christ be emptied of its power' (1:17, italics added).
- 'And so it was with me, brothers and sisters. When I came to you, I did not come with *eloquence* or human wisdom as I proclaimed to you the testimony about God' (2:1, italics added).

According to Paul we have to pick a side and not allow ourselves to be deceived by current trends:

Do not deceive yourselves. If any of you think you are wise by the standards of this age, you should become 'fools' so that you may become wise. For the wisdom of this world is foolishness in God's sight. As it is written: 'He catches the wise in their craftiness'; and again, 'The Lord knows that the thoughts of the wise are futile.' So then, no more boasting about human leaders! (3:18–21)

So it is manipulative rhetoric that is the target for Paul, not the use of the mind. This is also seen in a number of places in the letter, where Paul actually *encourages* the Corinthians to use their minds:

- 'I speak to sensible people; judge for yourselves what I say' (10:15).
- 'I will pray with my spirit, but I will also pray with my understanding; I will . . . sing with my understanding' (14:15).
- 'Brothers and sisters, stop thinking like children. In regard to evil be infants, but in your thinking be adults' (14:20).

In fact, right through the letter Paul is *arguing* his case. For example, in chapter 6, he again and again reminds his readers of knowledge he assumes they have and of the consequences they should be ready to draw: '[D]o you not know?' (v. 2); 'Do you not know?' (v. 3); 'Do you not know?' (v. 15); 'Do you not know?' (v. 16); 'Do you not know?' (v. 19). This all presupposes the use of the mind.

To sum up: Should we interpret Putin's gait as a signal of weakness or of strength? Should we understand Paul in 1 Corinthians to say that the gospel is foolish or wise? With the historical background in Corinth the picture falls into place. As Anthony Thiselton says in his commentary:

what we now know of the rhetorical background at Corinth, releases Paul of any hint of an uncharacteristic or obsessional *anti-intellectualism*, or any lack of imagination or *communicative flexibility*. His settled resolve was that he would do only what served the gospel . . . regardless of people's expectations or seductive shortcuts to success, most of all the seduction of self-advertisement. Neither then nor now does the gospel rest on the magnetism of 'big personalities.'[12]

Two Kinds of Wisdom and Two Kinds of Foolishness

Paul not only discusses the concepts of foolishness and wisdom in his letter; he speaks of *different* kinds of foolishness, *different* kinds of wisdom. And he claims that the gospel constitutes *true wisdom from God*.

The text is full of irony. Foolishness passes for wisdom, and wisdom is cast aside as if it were foolishness. Humanity believes itself to be wise and calls God a fool. But the greatest 'foolishness' of God surpasses the greatest human 'wisdom'. In this situation it is important to be able to distinguish between false wisdom and true wisdom, between human/worldly wisdom and the wisdom of God:

False wisdom	True wisdom
• wisdom and eloquence (1:17)	• wisdom among the mature (2:6)
• wisdom of the wise (1:19)	• wisdom from God (1:30)
• wisdom of the world (1:20)	• God's wisdom, a mystery (2:7)
• eloquence or human wisdom (2:1)	• Christ crucified . . . the wisdom
• human wisdom (2:13)	of God (1:23–24)

Paul is not critical of wisdom. On the contrary, it is wisdom that he advocates. What he rejects is 'the wisdom of the world' and 'human wisdom'. When Paul says that 'the message of the cross is foolishness', he makes clear that the message is not intellectually inferior. The sentence continues, 'to those who are perishing' (1:18). The text refers to those people who reject the gospel's *claim that it is foolish*, something of which Paul was well aware. Mistakenly expecting a Messiah who was politically successful, Jews rejected the gospel about a crucified Messiah. By the same token, Greeks – who were searching for philosophical ideas that could capture reality – also rejected the gospel (1:22–23). But the problem is not the gospel but rather their misconceptions about it. In itself the gospel is not foolish: it is 'the power of God and the wisdom of God' (1:24).[13]

Notes

1. Bible quotations in this chapter are from the New International Version (2011 ed.).

2. Aristotle, *Metaphysics* 4.7.

3. William Ramsay, *St. Paul the Traveller and the Roman Citizen* (London: Hodder & Stoughton, 1892), p. 252.

4. *The Guardian*, 16 December 2015 <https://www.theguardian.com/world/2015/dec/16/putin-gunslinger-gait-kgb-training-report>.

5. <http://www.svd.se/forskare-kgb-traning-bakom-putins-gang#sida-2>.

6. Dio Chrysostom, *Discourses* 8.5, Loeb Classical Library (Cambridge, Mass.: Harvard University Press, 1940).

7. Philostratus, *The Lives of the Sophists* (Cambridge, Mass.: Harvard University Press 1961), pp. xix–xx.

8. Dio Chrysostom, *Discourses* 32.10.

9. Plutarch, *Makers of Rome – Nine Lives* (London: Guild, 1993), p. 272.

10. Bruce Winter, *Philo and Paul Among the Sophists* (Grand Rapids, Mich.: Eerdmans, 2002), p. 55.

11. <http://www.patheos.com/blogs/bibleandculture/2012/08/20/paul-thru-mediterranean-eyes-a-review-part-three>.

12. Anthony Thiselton, *The First Epistle to the Corinthians* (Grand Rapids, Mich.: Eerdmans; Carlisle: Paternoster, 2000), p. 212 (italics original).

13. Many thanks to Agnes Rysinska for her help with translation into English.

5. APOLOGETICS – ALWAYS READY

Kirsten Birkett

I have been invited to write about apologetics in honour of Don
Carson: a pleasure and a privilege, to write on behalf of a friend so
committed to using his learning for the glory of God and the service
of God's people. Being familiar with Don's works on apologetics,
through his writing and speaking, I can hope only to add a small
footnote of appreciation. Writing this chapter has, however, proved
a curious task. I must admit that, in the course of writing it, I have
discovered that I am not at all sure that apologetics exists.

This might seem odd, since many people might think that I have
spent a lot of my adult life doing apologetics. I have written and
spoken on proofs for the existence of God, miracles, science,
feminism, culture and world views. In the course of teaching philosophy, ethics and (yes) apologetics, I have taught students how to
understand ideas in the secular world and respond to them, how
to start conversations and how to answer particular questions. Surely
I was doing something that exists.

Maybe that is a bit strong. Of course it exists: people do it. Don
Carson does it extremely well. But what are they doing? What is this
practice that has involved Christians throughout the centuries, that

has produced such an immense body of writing and theory about
its writing? When we claim that a book is a work of apologetics, or
put on lecture series or appoint professors in apologetics, just what
are they meant to do? In particular, how is this distinct from anything
else that Christians do?

In common parlance, at least, apologetics seems to be something
with a distinct audience as well as a distinct method. The audience
is usually meant to be unbelievers; the method, argument or reason,
to persuade them to drop their objections to Christianity. It is
generally considered a precursor to evangelism, distinguished from
evangelism because it involves reason rather than proclamation of
the gospel. It is generally also thought of as a different thing from
preaching, or 'theology', because it is addressed to non-believers
rather than believers.[1]

Yet how well will these distinctions stand up to scrutiny? When
Paul spoke to the Athenians in his famous address of Acts 17, was
he not doing theology: describing truths of God, albeit those that
were of particular relevance to his Athenian audience? How is this
essentially different from Romans, or the letters to the Corinthians,
or indeed any of the New Testament?

The issue gets more intricate still. In the metaliterature on apologetics we also see a great deal of discussion of the best way to go
about it. As in any discipline, different schools of thought have
emerged. If we can simplify the schools of apologetics current at
the moment, we might say that the big debate is between what are
sometimes called 'traditional' and 'presuppositional' schools. On
the traditional side are those that appeal to some kind of common
or neutral ground to argue for the reasonableness of the Christian
faith. Whether this starts with logic and the rational proofs for the
existence of God, or whether it goes straight to historical evidences
for Jesus and the reliability of the New Testament, the point of the
argument is that Christian belief is reasonable, indeed compelling.

The newer alternative to this general approach came to fruition
during the twentieth century (although in some ways it could be
traced back through the Reformation to Augustine) and uses the
language of world views and presuppositions. Every system of
thought – every world view – it is argued, rests on assumed premises
that make up its presuppositions. For any system, conclusions should

follow from premises in a logical way. However, a system based on non-Christian premises will necessarily fail at some point, for its premises are just not true; the task for the apologist is to point out at which point any particular system will find itself failing, involving self-contradiction or something at odds with reality. This can indeed be a very enlightening method for prosecuting a case against a non-Christian system of thought, while promoting Christianity.

However, this debate about method can quickly merge into a discussion not just of what is the best *way of doing* apologetics, but also of just what a person is *doing at all* when engaged in this task. The classical or traditional approach tends to see apologetics as engaging the non-Christian in a common quest for truth. So I, as the Christian believer, humbly put myself alongside the seeking unbeliever, and we discuss together what we can know as true. I put the case for Christianity, using evidences, logic or whatever tool I see is appropriate: even (I suppose) a comparison of presuppositions in a form of argument to the best explanation. Together, for the sake of the exercise, we put aside the assumption that any one conclusion *must* be true, and see where we get to.

On the other hand, presuppositionalism – when it is presented not just as a useful method, but as a theory of apologetics – sees this as not just inaccurate, but also unchristian. Presuppositionalists argue doctrinally that there is no such thing as neutral ground; indeed, it is entirely unscriptural to suggest that there is. The only legitimate way for a Christian to argue, then, is from the standpoint of Christian presuppositions, using scripturally endorsed criteria for rationality and judgement.[2] To suggest to an unbelieving conversation partner that it is ever possible to start from neutral ground is dishonest and blasphemous.

With such variation, and indeed strong language, from both 'sides', it is not surprising that suspicions abound in both directions. If we try to argue from some kind of common ground, using methods of argument and assumptions that can be agreed upon by a non-Christian, do we concede ground to unbelief and pander to a delusional world? Is this giving in to unbiblical thought, propagating lies to non-Christians and participating in idolatry? On the other hand, if we start from Christian assumptions – for instance, from a stance of biblical authority – do we make ourselves foolish and fail to connect with people? Is that just Bible-thumping and soapbox ranting?

My goodness. How heated a simple discussion can become. It seems not only that we do not really know what we are doing, but when we do it, we are in danger of either foolishness or idolatry. Should we engage in apologetics at all?

Apologetics: Don't Do It

I have certainly come across strong opposition to the idea of apologetics, not just from non-Christians who (understandably) do not wish to have their positions criticized, but also from within evangelical circles: from people who, one might think, should be in favour of defending the faith. However, it seems that the objection stems from just this impulse. What we should do, the argument runs, is evangelism. Evangelism, pure and simple. Proclaim the gospel, tell the world the saving message of Jesus. The gospel saves; argument does not. Reason cannot get us to God; that is tantamount to saying our works can save us. We are irretrievably fallen, darkened in our minds, and we need the light of the gospel to shine upon us. Messing around with logical argument avoids the real issue: people need Jesus. So give them Jesus.

As it has been presented to me, this view often comes with the backing of Paul's words in 1 Corinthians: 'Jews demand signs and Greeks seek wisdom, but we preach Christ crucified, a stumbling block to Jews and folly to Gentiles' (1:22–23).[3]

Engaging in apologetics, it would seem, is to behave like the unbelieving Greeks, seeking worldly wisdom. No, we should instead be preaching Christ crucified. After all, that is what Paul did, and what he goes on to say in chapter 2 just reinforces this:

> And I, when I came to you, brothers, did not come proclaiming to you the testimony of God with lofty speech or wisdom. For I decided to know nothing among you except Jesus Christ and him crucified. And I was with you in weakness and in fear and much trembling, and my speech and my message were not in plausible words of wisdom, but in demonstration of the Spirit and of power, that your faith might not rest in the wisdom of men but in the power of God. (2:1–5)

We must not seek the 'plausible words of wisdom'; this would lead people to rest in the wisdom of men. No, we should know nothing but Jesus Christ and him crucified, which is the power of God. Case closed.

It is a strong case and caused me considerable heartache as an undergraduate: Was I indeed capitulating to worldly wisdom in wanting to find good arguments for the validity of Christianity? Was I in thrall to plausible words of wisdom when I tried to argue with my fellow students and teachers about the existence of God or the validity of Scripture?

It was Scripture itself that provided the answer. In Scripture we see the apostle Paul both explaining and demonstrating just how to go about preaching Christ and him crucified. Even in the Areopagus, that stronghold of the wisdom-seeking Greeks, Paul presented his preaching of Christ crucified as part of a sustained argument. Taking a point of local interest, the altar to the unknown God, Paul moves to the nature of God as creator, our relationship to him, the foolishness of idolatry and the necessity of repentance because of judgment. Christ's resurrection from the dead is the culmination of this argument, the grounds on which Paul argues that his call to repentance is justified (Acts 17:22–31).

This is evidently typical of Paul's pattern of preaching to Gentiles. He had already spent time in Athens reasoning with those in the marketplace (17:17), conversing with the Epicurean and Stoic philosophers: not simply pandering to the fashion for wanting to play with new ideas, but using the curiosity about ideas for the sake of presenting the truth. Moreover, it was effective: as well as those who mocked, several believed (17:34). Similarly, when preaching Christ crucified to Jews, we see Paul 'proving' that Jesus is the Christ (Acts 9:22), 'reasoning' from the Scriptures, 'explaining' and 'proving' his points (Acts 17:2–3), and persuading some (see also Acts 26:28–29; 28:23–24).

Paul was certainly not the only New Testament figure to do so. In fact, wherever we see the gospel proclaimed in the New Testament, by Jesus or others, we see supporting arguments and evidences; miracles were by no means the only source of validation of the message. Jesus' own 'repent and believe in the gospel' is a conclusion, following from his reasons: 'The time is fulfilled, and the kingdom of God is at hand' (Mark 1:15). John 20:30–31 tells us that the Gospel was written 'so that you may believe' and by believing 'have life'; the whole book is meant to persuade readers to faith.

As we see the gospel spread, and read the letters to the churches that result, we see an engagement with the mind as Christ crucified is preached reasonably. The letter to the Romans contains sustained propositional logic, as do sections of Paul's other letters. Hebrews argues persuasively from Old Testament practices to the significance and superiority of Jesus. Peter's exhortations come in logical sequence. John argues perhaps more elliptically in his letters but no less in logical form. The apostles never capitulate to an empty love of wisdom; but they do use the best of wisdom to commend the gospel to their hearers.

But Is This Apologetics?

So it seems that biblically, at least, there is no strong distinction between various word-related activities, as the apostles spread the news of the gospel and commended it to their hearers. Perhaps it was afterwards that the distinctions arose?

Well, no, not really. Take, for instance, *The Apology of Aristides the Philosopher*. This is addressed to the emperor Hadrian, an unbeliever, so perhaps here we have a classic example of apologetics proper: defending the gospel against the objections of the unbeliever. Indeed, this treatise contains direct criticism of opposing systems of belief, those who worship things of nature as gods, as well as Greek, Egyptian and Jewish religion. It also contains a direct defence of Christianity against specific accusations of immorality. If apologetics is distinct from evangelism, however, this tract hardly qualifies, *Apology* or not: it preaches judgment coming through Jesus and ends with what might be considered a straightforward altar call. Is this preaching, evangelism or apologetics? It could be labelled all three.

Similarly, Irenaeus in *Against Heresies* certainly addresses unbelievers, in his extensive description and rebuttal of Gnosticism. This is followed by a careful presentation of the Christian faith, in which he describes the covenantal plan of God and connection between the Old and New Testaments. This is surely theology –

indeed, it could be considered an early systematic theology – but Irenaeus is known as an apologist because he was writing to oppose heretics.

Justin Martyr, perhaps the most famous of ancient 'apologists', was certainly no stranger to reason and the use of philosophy in his writing. Far from it: in his *Dialogue with Trypho*, a defence of Christianity as addressed to the Jewish community, he describes how he became a believer because Christianity was presented to him as the true philosophy that answers all his questions. He considered philosophy 'the knowledge of that which really exists, and a clear perception of the truth; and happiness is the reward of such knowledge and wisdom'. He wrote that when presented with Christianity, 'I found this philosophy alone to be safe and profitable':

> Thus, and for this reason, I am a philosopher. Moreover, I would wish that all, making a resolution similar to my own, do not keep themselves away from the words of the Saviour. For they possess a terrible power in themselves, and are sufficient to inspire those who turn aside from the path of rectitude with awe; while the sweetest rest is afforded those who make a diligent practice of them. If, then, you have any concern for yourself, and if you are eagerly looking for salvation, and if you believe in God, you may – since you are not indifferent to the matter – become acquainted with the Christ of God, and, after being initiated, live a happy life.[4]

Justin goes on in the dialogue to demonstrate to Trypho, a Jew, why Jesus is the Christ and how he fulfils the Old Testament. Stephen did a similar thing before his martyrdom; Peter was engaged on a similar task in Acts 2; and we can imagine that Paul may well have spoken to the Jews thus as he reasoned with them in the synagogues, proving that Jesus is the Christ. An impassioned presentation of the gospel, full of theological content, with argument, assuming the truth of Christianity but appealing to the common ground of philosophy, does not fall easily into our modern categories.

Still, we might say, these early Christians were still working out how best to think and write about Christianity. The clearer distinctions we draw between different types of Christian intellectual activity took time to emerge. It is true that, as time goes on, we see more distinct types of Christian writing developing. While Augustine's

On the Trinity does all the things that theology and apologetics do, it is not addressed to the world in the same way that *The City of God* is. By the time we enter the Middle Ages, the nature of Christian engagement with its own ideas and those of the world has changed greatly from the time of the earlier church. This was very much affected by cultural and political developments. Once you have Christendom, a largely assumed Christian culture, the need for apologetics against non-Christians becomes much more specific and very clearly addressed to outsiders. Our heroes of the Reformation, too, did not much address non-Christian unbelief: they were addressing wrong theology, all of which at least purported to be Christian. Calvin's Geneva College did not have courses on apologetics. It did, however, have courses on literature, and the language instruction was given through classical, not biblical, texts. Is it the prevailing culture, then, that is most important in considering apologetics? Is apologetics not an eternal category as much as a response to whatever the surrounding culture presents?

Apologetics Deals with Culture

Perhaps we are now coming closer to what we *really* mean by creating a distinct category of 'apologetics'. Christian apologetic writing, whatever else it does, also addresses prevailing culture, either defending from particular contemporary criticisms, or providing cultural critique or explanation. This is, indeed, quite a profound thing to do, and provides a very strong defence of the faith for both Christians and non-Christians. A system of thought that can not only stand up against attacks from other systems, not only provide solid defence for its own theses, but in turn explains the opposition, is a strong system indeed. Aristides, Justin Martyr, and Augustine in *City of God* did not just provide a *critique* of non-Christian culture but also a theological *explanation* for it. Christians need an understanding of their world, and apologetics, like theology, is always situated. The truths are eternal, but as soon as they are articulated they are spoken sometime, to someone. So perhaps what we want to say is that while apologetics is always in some sense a defence of the gospel, how the gospel is defended (method), and from what it is defended (content), change over time.

Whatever the idolatry of the moment, it will need to be addressed, in order to challenge unbelief both inside and outside the church. It will change from age to age, but our stance towards it – challenging untruth with biblical truth – will not. This would suggest that, even if content and method are variable, there are still certain unchanging rules about apologetics. First, following apologists from the early church through to the Reformation and beyond, we need to know our culture. Like Irenaeus who engaged so fully with the Gnostics, we need to understand the arguments of our opponents, in their own terms, seeing what makes these appealing to them. We take seriously the fact that Calvin wanted his students to be well educated in Aristotle, Plato, Plutarch and Cicero, Greek poets, orators and historiographers, and natural philosophy, as well as the Scriptures and doctrine. We understand that preaching, teaching, evangelism and defence of the faith must address real people and their understanding, whatever that is.

There is another unchanging rule. If the method of apologetics might change depending on what the prevailing culture needs, the manner does not. Biblically, we know that our speech to outsiders must be gracious, as if seasoned with salt (Col. 4:6). We must hold firmly to the fact that apologetics – however reasoned, however immersed in non-Christian thought and its philosophical method – is *never* simply an intellectual exercise. Apologetics is a manifestation of love. It demonstrates that we love God, and want above all to see him glorified; that we love truth, and want to promote truth over falsehood; and that we love people, and wish to see them moved from death to life. The truth about God matters, and it is crucial to love of others that we care what they believe. We are dealing in eternal consequences.

It is important that we include this in any discussion of apologetics, for it is all too easy for those with a love of ideas and intellectual debate to forget that truth is never abstract. It must certainly never be separate from love of people; that way the Inquisition lies. When we destroy arguments and every lofty opinion raised against the knowledge of God, we remember that Paul says this in the context of not boasting (2 Cor. 10). His love for those he reasoned with and argued with and taught is always evident (1 Thess. 2:8). Our defence of the hope that is in us is always given with gentleness and respect (1 Peter 3:15). May I add that Don Carson has always been an astonishingly good example of this in practice.

Twenty-First-Century Apologetics: Where Are We Now?

As I read the early apologists, I am disturbingly conscious that all too soon, even in the Western world, we may well find ourselves before the rulers of the land, defending, if not perhaps our lives, at least our freedom to be active Christians. We may find that 'apologetics' returns to its original legal context. There are many parts of the world in which such demands are a current reality.

At the same time, we continue our intellectual defence of the faith against the prevailing philosophies that would challenge it. Postmodernism is probably here to stay for a while longer; it is no longer exciting, just assumed from school to pub to newspaper to university. At the same time, modernism still matters; science still not only commands a huge part of public authority, but empirical thinking and an anti-authoritarian stance to knowledge sit alongside postmodernism in uneasy juxtaposition. Even educated thinkers can switch between modern and postmodern worlds bafflingly fast. The physicist who will be absolutely hard-nosed as she evaluates data from the Large Hadron Collider might be full of semi-mystical feeling as she considers her ecological good deeds. 'Nobody imagined [Sir James] Frazer actually *practising* magic,' an academic historian writes, 'but these days your new junior colleague might be a witch.'[5]

The problem of entitlement is often noted as a current challenge to evangelism: as well as this, and intimately connected, is the problem of apathy. No amount of familiarity with philosophical argument, proofs for God, knowledge of fine-tuning of the universe, or world-view critique matters when people simply do not care. It is not so much that we come across arguments against Christianity, or even the other new Western problem of almost complete biblical ignorance; it is simply that no one wants to be bothered thinking about it at all. Whether materially comfortable or struggling, consistent thinkers or entirely fragmented, there is a growing generation of those who cannot be bothered. Here, I would suggest, it is not argument that is needed so much as patience: patient relationship, waiting for the moment when attention is engaged. Is this apologetics? It is still being ready to give a reason for a hope, when, eventually, that hope is noticed. It might just take a long time.

Are We Exalting Reason in Doing Apologetics?

Conservative believers today do not exalt reason in the Kantian sense, nor do they deny the authority of Scripture. However, many will still assume that 'apologetics' – the defence of the gospel – is something that uses only reason, and they fear that. We need not. Reason is not absolute, nor is it necessary to believe so to do apologetics. After all, Scripture is reasonable; it is people who are not. Sin, as Augustine recognized so long ago, corrupts the will. It is not that human minds are intrinsically incapable of grasping the truths of God; created in God's image, human minds are capable of understanding all sorts of truth. However we do not *want* the truths of God, the truths that require our obedient submission to him. Our corrupted wills darken our minds, and only God's Spirit can change that. Becoming a Christian, entering the mind of Christ and apprehending spiritual truths does not mean becoming less rational; it means becoming *more* rational. The secular god Reason is a poor second to the real reason that God's Spirit opens for us. The created god can bring us only to selfish and lesser truths, which might tell us a lot about how the natural world works and how clever we are within it, but will never lead us to salvation from sin and eternal life. Only the true wisdom that comes from the Spirit allows that.

So we set forth Christian truth, knowing that it is reasonable, even if unspiritual minds cannot yet see it. We apply that Christian truth to our culture, knowing that a gospel critique will uncover profound realities and important criticisms. We attack particular unchristian absurdities, hoping that even unenlightened reason might have enough humility to accept that particular smokescreens have been blown away. We argue, and persuade, and speak into whatever context we can find, becoming a Jew to Jews and a Greek to Greeks, making sure we understand the science of scientists and the art of artists, the anger of atheists and the play of postmoderns, the deep love for creation of the environmentalist and the longing for spiritual wisdom of the New Ager, so that by all means we might win some. When the ideas of Christianity are attacked we defend them, explaining what they are and why they are not to be dismissed. We appeal to minds and wills and hearts, all the time praying that God's Spirit might change these so they can come to truth. When we can, we proclaim the most important truth of all, the saving news that Jesus has died to pay for sins so that there is no condemnation, but new life through his resurrection. And then we do it all over again.

The apostle Peter told us to be ready always to make a defence of our hope (1 Peter 3:15). That verse is frequently cited as the biblical basis for apologetics. I would like to add another one:

> preach the word; be ready in season and out of season; reprove, rebuke, and exhort, with complete patience and teaching. For the time is coming when people will not endure sound teaching, but having itching ears they will accumulate for themselves teachers to suit their own passions, and will turn away from listening to the truth and wander off into myths. (2 Tim. 4:2–4)

The myths will change, but our job does not. The patience will always be necessary, as will the truth be. God's word will go forth, using us as his servants. We can ask for no better task.

Notes

1. These are the distinctions that most 'ordinary' Christians hold: people who write books on the theory of apologetics generally make their definitions more broad. Yet the very fact that we still have books (and courses of study) published on 'apologetics', as distinct from evangelism, doctrine, preaching or some other category, suggests that the narrower definitions are the ones that still hold in the general Christian consciousness.
2. See the discussion in ch. 1 of John Frame, *Apologetics: A Justification of Christian Belief* (Phillipsburg, N.J.: Presbyterian & Reformed, 2015).
3. Bible quotations in this chapter are from the English Standard Version.

4. Justin Martyr, *Dialogue with Trypho*, ch. 8, in Alexander Roberts and James Donaldson (eds.), *The Ante-Nicene Fathers: Translations of the Writings of the Fathers down to A.D. 325* (Edinburgh: T&T Clark, 1996), vol. 1, p. 198.

5. Christopher I. Lehrich, 'Magic in Theoretical Practice', in Bernd-Christian Otto and Michael Stausberg (eds.), *Defining Magic: A Reader* (Sheffield: Equinox, 2013), p. 212, italics original.

6. GOSPEL COOPERATION WITHOUT COMPROMISE

John Stevens

It is a great privilege to be invited to contribute to this collection of essays in honour of Professor Carson. I was converted as a law student at Cambridge University in 1988, and it would be no under-statement to say that Don Carson, through his books and Bible ministry at numerous conferences in the UK over the last thirty years, has been the single most important theological influence on me and my ministry. I own more books by him than by any other single author. His commentary *The Gospel According to John*[1] was one of the first I bought as a young Christian and introduced me to the importance of exegetical rigour and clarity. *Showing the Spirit*[2] helped me to navigate the controversies swirling around the charismatic movement at that time, and *The Gagging of God*[3] protected me from the onslaughts of postmodernism. *How Long O Lord*[4] taught me about God's sovereignty and human responsibility and *A Call to Spiritual Reformation*[5] taught me to pray with biblical priorities. *Exegetical Fallacies*[6] has saved me from many foolish errors in my preaching, and more recently the *Commentary on the New Testament Use of the Old Testament*[7] has proved an invaluable resource of insight-ful and balanced biblical theology.

Nearly thirty years after my conversion, I find myself, much to my own surprise, the National Director of the Fellowship of Independent Evangelical Churches (FIEC), a family of over 560 churches in Great Britain that are committed to working together to make disciples of Jesus Christ in every community. To this end we seek to grow gospel-driven churches to reach Britain for Christ.[8] We are a group of churches that are united by core gospel doctrines and convictions, but that permits a wide variety of views on other, secondary matters, and encompasses a range of styles and cultures of local-church ministry. We also want to work more widely with other churches that share our gospel convictions, irrespective of their denominational affiliation. We seek to maintain gospel clarity on what is essential and gospel generosity on everything else. We believe that this reflects the teaching of the New Testament.

Although FIEC was founded back in 1922, we owe a huge debt of gratitude to Don Carson for the way in which he has modelled gospel cooperation between evangelicals across denominational boundaries. No one has done more to foster gospel-centred unity than he has over the past thirty years. In 2007 I was privileged to attend a gathering of the FIEC Pastors' Association at Cheltenham Bible Festival, where Don spoke on the origins, aims and structure of The Gospel Coalition (TGC),[9] which was then in its infancy. For those who had ears to hear, his message was loud and clear: if we are to meet the multiple challenges facing evangelicalism in the early twenty-first century in the West, we need to avoid unnecessary factionalism and stand together on the core truths of the gospel. Evangelicalism, which has always been a pandenominational movement, needs a 'centre' around which to gather, determined by the historic doctrines and convictions that have defined it. Over the last ten years TGC has become a bastion of evangelical orthodoxy, a source of outstanding resources and an embodiment of gospel cooperation, as leaders from a wide range of denominations, including Presbyterians, Baptists, Independents and Episcopalians, have joined together, whether as Council members, conference speakers or supporters. Don's address at Cheltenham Bible Festival has informed and inspired the vision of FIEC to unite Independent churches in Great Britain around a gospel 'centre', and to partner with like-minded evangelicals in other cross-denominational ministries and organizations.

It is also highly appropriate that I am writing this chapter in 2016, almost exactly fifty years after the fateful disagreement between Dr Martyn Lloyd-Jones and the Revd John Stott at the National Assembly of Evangelicals in London in October 1966. This much misunderstood event, at which it has often been wrongly perceived that Lloyd-Jones called evangelicals to leave their mixed denominations,[10] marked the beginning of a significant rupture of gospel unity between evangelical Anglicans and evangelical nonconformists in the UK, which has taken decades to heal.[11] That healing process has been in no small measure helped by the way in which Don Carson has been able to build bridges between different constituencies within UK conservative evangelicalism, all of whom hold him in the highest regard for his biblical fidelity. He has ministered at the Proclamation Trust, Gospel Partnerships, FIEC, Grace Baptists, Evangelical Movement of Wales, Word Alive and UCCF, to name but a few. Unity between Bible-centred evangelicals in the UK is stronger than it has ever been in my Christian lifetime, for which I and the FIEC rejoice.

However, the challenges facing evangelicals in the UK today are potentially greater than they were in 1966, and require us to have an even greater clarity about the gospel and even stronger commitment to gospel cooperation. In 1966 the primary challenge was liberal theology and the pressure of the ecumenical movement, which sought to unify churches structurally into a single denomination, without concern for confessional orthodoxy. Lloyd-Jones was therefore right to highlight that the key issue at stake was 'What is a Christian?' Today there are fewer overt liberals, and the challenge comes from those who profess to be evangelicals but who are rejecting historic evangelical beliefs about the Bible, the cross, judgment, sexuality and gender, to name but a few contemporary pressure points. In 1966 the challenge came from those who directly denied the truth of the Bible. Today the challenge comes from those who claim to honour its authority and yet interpret it in such a way that it means exactly the opposite of what evangelicals have always held it to mean. If old-style liberalism can be compared to the big bad wolf who wanted to blow the whole house down, then the self-proclaimed contemporary evangelicals who are reinterpreting core biblical beliefs are more like Lewis Carroll's Humpty Dumpty, making words mean what they want them to mean.

The rejection-through-reinterpretation of historic evangelical beliefs, coupled with the sweeping secularization of society, which has left Christians a marginalized minority whose historic convictions are viewed as little short of intolerant bigotry, will inevitably force evangelicals to take a stand. They will have to decide what they believe, who they can join with in gospel work, and who they can associate with as brothers and sisters in Christ. As denominations, churches and parachurch organizations determine their policies on, for example, same-sex marriages and homosexuality, evangelicals will have no option but to decide whether they will capitulate, compromise, contend for the truth or come out from among them.

In such times it is essential that we seek to draw the boundaries of gospel cooperation biblically, and that we do so in advance of the specific challenges that we might face. It is always more difficult to determine boundaries reactively, especially when to do so might mean excluding and rejecting former friends and colleagues in ministry. Imposing boundaries reactively and responsively will always run the risk of looking harsh, uncompassionate and reactionary. Only if we have a clear centre, and have identified the necessary boundaries, can we make the judgements that will inevitably follow. This chapter will sketch the biblical grounds for gospel cooperation, and also the limits to such cooperation.

What Is the Gospel? The Essential Prerequisites for Cooperation without Compromise

Fundamental to gospel cooperation is the very question of what the gospel is in the first place. Only if this can be determined with some precision will it be possible to identify teaching and practice that are beyond the bounds.

Those who profess to be evangelicals can fall into two opposite dangers. On the one hand, there are those who view the 'gospel' in a maximalist way, as encompassing everything that they believe the Bible has to say. For them, 'gospel' is virtually synonymous with 'biblical' and encompasses a plethora of issues such as eschatology and ecclesiology. It dictates not just doctrine but styles of worship and cultures of ministry. Where 'gospel' is taken in such a maximalist way, gospel cooperation will be possible only between those who share every conviction in common. On the other hand, there are those who do not seem to regard the gospel as having any doctrinal content other than the vaguest confession of Jesus as Lord. They adopt a minimalist approach that affirms all those who take upon themselves the name of 'Christian', irrespective of what they mean by it.

The New Testament teaching clearly lies between these extremes. The 'gospel' is the verbal message announcing the good news about Jesus, who he is and what he has done, which demands that people respond in repentance and faith to escape the wrath to come.[12] The gospel therefore has an irreducible minimum doctrinal content, which is utterly non-negotiable. At the same time, it does not encompass the totality of biblical teaching.

The irreducible content of the gospel is expressed nowhere more succinctly than in 1 Corinthians 15:1–8, where Paul reminds the church of the gospel that he had preached to them when he planted and established the church. This gospel, and this gospel alone, will save them, with the implication that a gospel that denies any of these core truths cannot bring salvation. The essence of the apostolic gospel, expressed in highly condensed language full of meaning, is that the historic person of Jesus of Nazareth was the Christ, the long promised, anointed King who would come to save God's people and fulfil the Old Testament promises. He gave his life as a propitiatory and substitutionary sacrifice when he 'died for our sins'.[13] On the third day he was raised from the dead, which (as the rest of ch. 15 makes clear) was a bodily resurrection into the life of the glorious age to come, which Paul characterizes as a 'spiritual body'.[14] This glorious resurrection both confirms that Jesus was the promised Christ/Messiah, and also reveals his full glory and divinity as the Son of God. It declares his ontological equality with God the Father.[15] The gospel also presupposes the doctrine of creation that Paul has already elucidated in chapter 8.[16]

These core truths formed the substance of the apostolic preaching in the book of Acts. While they may not be given the same emphasis in each of the major sermons recorded there,[17] they are always the substance of the message, whether explicitly or by implication. The subtle differences are a consequence of the contextualization of gospel preaching to various cultures. Jesus' identity as Lord and Christ, his death for sins that brings forgiveness, and his resurrection to glory and his return to judge are the irreducible minimum of apostolic gospel preaching.

It inevitably follows that there can be no gospel cooperation with those who deny these basic truths. Where they are denied, or simply downplayed, the message that is proclaimed is not the gospel, and consequently it will not bring salvation. As Paul so bluntly expresses it in Galatians 2:9, those who preach a different message are under the curse of God.

In the contemporary context the core apostolic conviction that is most often denied by self-professed evangelicals is that of the propitiatory, substitutionary sacrifice of Christ for our sins.[18] This doctrine, which permeates the entire New Testament, presupposes that the universal human problem is sin, the wrath of God that this rightly provokes and the eternal judgment that it justly deserves. This doctrine is openly denied by some, but more subtly displaced by others in favour of alternative models of the atonement that speak of Jesus' absorbing human evil and wickedness in an abstract sense, rather than taking upon himself the wrath of his Father in our place. While the New Testament presents various 'models' of the atonement, which together elucidate what Christ has accomplished by his death on our behalf, there is no choice to be made between them. Propitiatory, substitutionary atonement is the heart of the cross, and without it all the other 'models' of the atonement fail.[19] Gospel cooperation cannot be founded solely on what is mutually affirmed, but demands full consensus on what must not be denied.

It is for this reason that the doctrine of the cross has proved to be so central to evangelical unity and gospel cooperation.[20] Where there is disagreement as to the significance of Christ's death on the cross, either as to what took place when he died or as to the finished nature of his sacrifice, there can be no gospel cooperation because there is no gospel in common.

1 Corinthians 15:1–8 not only establishes an irreducible content of the gospel, which is a prerequisite for gospel cooperation, but

implicitly requires a common acceptance of the truthfulness and authority of the Bible. Paul explicitly demands acceptance of the Old Testament Scriptures, as the death and resurrection of Jesus were both 'according to the Scriptures'. However, he implicitly demands equal acceptance of the authority and truthfulness of the New Testament. The gospel he has proclaimed is the true gospel because it comes with his apostolic authority. It is consistent with the testimony of all the other apostles, who also saw the risen Lord Jesus. Ultimately it is not Paul's message, still less his opinion or interpretation. It is the message of the Lord Jesus that has been revealed to Paul[21] and the other apostles. The authority of the New Testament is rooted in its apostolicity, which places it on an equivalent basis with the Old Testament Scriptures.[22] By being written down, the apostolic teaching, revealed and authorized by the Lord Jesus, becomes authoritative Scripture. It has the same truthfulness and authority as the very word of God because it is the word of Jesus by his Spirit through his apostles.[23]

Gospel cooperation is therefore dependent upon a common acceptance of the truthfulness and authority of the Scriptures, as the word of God and the final authority over church tradition and human reason. As will be seen, this does not mean that there is no need for interpretation, nor that differences on some matters necessarily prevent gospel cooperation. But where there is no agreement on the formal authority of Scripture as the true and final word of God, there can be no scope for gospel cooperation.

Organizations such as FIEC,[24] TGC[25] and UCCF[26] have therefore adopted confessional statements that ground fellowship and cooperation on the basis of these core gospel truths, which have been the historic hallmark of evangelicalism.[27] They have encouraged cooperation between churches and Christians who hold very different views on other issues, but they demand commitment to the apostolic gospel as revealed in the Scriptures.

What Is False Teaching? The Essential Boundaries to Cooperation Without Compromise[28]

Having established that there is an irreducible minimum doctrinal content to the gospel that must not be denied, and which is therefore a prerequisite for gospel cooperation, the New Testament also makes clear that there are some people with whom we cannot fellowship, let alone join in gospel cooperation. These include those who teach a false gospel because they deny the fundamental truths outlined in 1 Corinthians 15, but extend beyond these to those who promote teaching that is incompatible with eternal salvation. The New Testament brands such people 'false teachers' and demands that faithful gospel believers, and especially leaders, separate from them. They are to be silenced in the churches and given no platform for their teaching. They are to be excluded from the community[29] because their beliefs and behaviour have made clear that they do not truly belong to the Lord Jesus and they have no place in his kingdom.[30] They need to repent.

The need to exercise such discipline, and to separate from false teachers, emerged in the course of the bitter divisions and doctrinal disputes that afflicted the early church, which originated as the gospel confronted the Jewish or pagan backgrounds of the first-generation converts to Christianity. A significant majority of the New Testament letters are taken up with tackling the problem of false teachings that are both contrary to the apostolic gospel and threaten to destroy the church. What might appear harsh and judgmental to many contemporary Western ears was rightly recognized as a matter of eternal life and death by the apostles. False teaching is not 'sound', meaning that it is unhealthy because it does not bring the blessing of eternal life.[31]

The New Testament identifies a number of specific examples of false teachings that require such discipline and rejection. They include the denial that Jesus is the Christ[32] or that he came in the flesh,[33] the denial of the bodily resurrection of Jesus, the denial of the resurrection to come for those who trust in Christ,[34] the denial of the second coming of Jesus to bring judgment and the kingdom.[35] False teaching also includes legalism that imposes the performance of any religious work, such as circumcision or observance of the Jewish dietary code, as a condition of salvation, thus undermining the doctrine of justification by faith alone.[36] It includes the imposition of asceticism, which demands abstention from marriage and eating certain foods,[37] and the promotion and practice of sexual immorality,[38] which encompasses all sexual activity outside heterosexual marriage. Finally, those who promote division in the church, or who reject apostolic authority, are also to be disciplined and excluded.[39]

Not every erroneous teaching is categorized as 'false teaching' in this way by the New Testament; in some surprising areas there is recognition that diverse approaches can be accommodated. Paul, for example, clearly regards the issue of Sabbath observance as a matter of personal conscience, even though it appears in the Ten Commandments. Individual Christians are therefore free to observe one day as more sacred than another, but also to consider every day alike.[40] Similarly Christians who have fully grasped the freedom they have in Christ to eat anything, including meat that may have been sacrificed to idols in a pagan temple, are to respect the consciences of their 'weaker' brothers and sisters who still feel obliged to observe the Jewish dietary restrictions.[41] The crucial issue in such circumstances is not what people choose to do, but that they do not require others to do the same as a condition for salvation, and that they do not condemn or look down on others for the different decisions of conscience they make.[42]

Taken together, therefore, the New Testament establishes that there are some doctrines that must be believed for gospel unity and cooperation to be possible, there are some teachings that are false and endanger salvation that prevent any fellowship at all, and there is a wide category between these two where a diversity of beliefs and practices can be accepted provided that they are not elevated to requirements for salvation. To put it in different taxonomical terminology, there are primary doctrines that must be believed, heretical beliefs that must be rejected and secondary beliefs where gospel cooperation is possible despite a diversity of beliefs and practices. The scope for gospel cooperation without compromise thus lies within both a centred and a bounded set. It occurs within a centred set that is focused on the core gospel doctrines, but it is limited to a bounded set that excludes those who are false teachers promoting dangerous doctrines. The FIEC, for example, has sought to recognize this by adopting a policy statement on *Gospel Unity* that encourages partnership in worship and evangelism with those who hold core gospel convictions, but rejects the possibility of such partnership with those who deny them.[43]

The most difficult question often appears to be that of determining where on this spectrum a particular issue might fall. To take a few contemporary examples, is it possible to enjoy gospel cooperation with those who differ over questions of ecclesiology, baptism, eschatology, women's ministry, baptism in the Spirit, charismatic gifts, Calvinistic or Arminian soteriology or the age of the earth? If gospel cooperation is possible despite differences on these issues, why is it not possible with those who differ on their understanding of the atonement or on issues of sexuality and same-sex marriage?

In reality the problem is nowhere near as difficult as might first appear. The core 'minimum' gospel doctrines of Jesus' deity, propitiatory death on the cross to bear the wrath of God against universal human sin, bodily resurrection, second coming, justification by faith alone and the truthfulness of the Bible will inevitably exclude the vast majority of false teachers who promote legalism or licence, because they will not subscribe to these basic beliefs either. Only a tiny number of people, for example, who profess to hold to the doctrine of the inerrancy of the Scriptures and propitiatory sacrifice also advocate the acceptance of same-sex relationships. The rejection of biblical sexual morality is usually preceded by rejection of the more foundational gospel doctrines. The core gospel doctrines, if they are rightly guarded, will generate a centred set that excludes most false teachers and will provide a sufficient basis for gospel cooperation.

Despite this, a sole focus on the central gospel doctrines is insufficient for cooperation. It remains necessary to try to identify other issues that constitute false teaching, not just so as to ensure gospel cooperation without compromise, but because they require the response of church discipline, and believers ought to separate themselves from those who teach them or allow them. The precise issues will vary from age to age and place to place, since they usually involve a clash between biblical teaching and the prevailing culture. In the New Testament era a major issue was that of sexual ethics, especially in respect of male sexual activity outside marriage, whether with slaves or prostitutes, which was deemed acceptable by pagan and Roman society.[44] Christians were to separate themselves from those who taught or practised such sexual immorality, or who taught against the enjoyment of sex within marriage, because they were thereby demonstrating that they were not truly converted.

However, while sexual sin was often the presenting issue, this was only one of a variety of sinful behaviours that were incompatible with true conversion and salvation, such that advocating or practising these sins would disqualify one from the kingdom of God. In 1 Corinthians 6:9–10 Paul lists sexual immorality, idolatry, adultery, homosexual sex, theft, greed, drunkenness, slander and swindling as patterns of behaviour that show that a person cannot inherit the kingdom of God. No doubt he would have demanded the discipline of, and separation from, anyone who was committing or advocating such sins who refused to repent.

What are the implications of this for us today? It ought to be clear that we cannot enter into gospel cooperation with those who reject the essential doctrines that define the gospel. It also means that we cannot enter into gospel cooperation with those who are false teachers, or the supporters of false teachers. This means, for example, that there can be no gospel cooperation with those who hold to the teaching of the Roman Catholic Church, which continues to deny the doctrine of salvation by grace alone through the finished work of Christ on the cross.[45] Similarly there can be no cooperation with fundamentalist legalists who insist that abstention from alcohol, dressing in a particular way, using a specific Bible translation or holding a particular eschatological view are essential to salvation. Nor can there be cooperation with a Messianic Jew who believes that it is necessary to be circumcised to receive salvation. Such legalism is, mercifully, rarely encountered in contemporary Britain, and those who hold such views would not wish to cooperate in any event. It is of much more contemporary relevance that these biblical principles mean that there cannot be cooperation with a person who believes that God accepts and affirms those who enter into loving and monogamous same-sex relationships.[46]

It is essential to recognize that a very wide range of issues fall between gospel essentials and heretical false teaching, and differences of belief about these issues ought not to make gospel cooperation impossible. Within this 'gospel space' brothers and sisters may disagree with one another, and have different beliefs and practices as a matter of conscience, yet they trust and proclaim the same saving gospel. Issues such as women's ordination, the age of the earth, whether the gift of tongues is for today, whether baptism is for professing believers or also for the children of believers, and whether Jesus' return will be post- or pre-millennial ought not to prevent gospel cooperation as a matter of principle. Such differences may make gospel cooperation difficult, or impractical for pragmatic reasons, but they do not make it impossible as a matter of theological principle. It would not be sinful and dangerous to cooperate across such divisions, whereas it would be sinful and dangerous to cooperate without unity on gospel essentials, or with those who teach or support heretical false teaching.

In contemporary culture, gospel cooperation requires both clarity and generosity. It requires clarity to stand firmly for the essential doctrines of the gospel and against false teaching and false teachers. There are far too many Christians who wrongly assume that we are called to accept everyone as they are, and to welcome all those who self-identify as Christians, no matter what they believe and practise. Jesus himself warned that there will be many people who self-identify as his disciples, naming him as Lord, yet do not truly know him because they do not obey his word.[47] As Paul explains in 1 Corinthians 5:1–8, to exercise discernment and discipline against those who deny the truth of the gospel, or who teach false doctrines, is ultimately an act of love. It is an act of love for God, as it seeks to honour his name and reputation in the world. It is an act of love for other Christians, as it will protect them from being led astray from salvation. It is an act of love for the false believers and false teachers, as it may prompt them to come to true repentance and salvation. The least loving thing we can do is simply to pretend that it does not matter.[48]

At the same time, gospel cooperation requires great generosity, and a refusal to elevate secondary matters to primary importance. Generosity means that we have to bear with the fact that others will do and teach things that we regard as wrong, unwise and unbiblical, yet we respect their consciences and stand together with them as brothers and sisters who hold the gospel in common.

What Is Gospel Generosity? The Essential Attitude for Cooperation Without Compromise

Having considered the prerequisites and limits of gospel cooperation we are finally in a position to consider what gospel cooperation might require in practice. This is a rather more complex question than might at first appear. We may choose to work with others in a wide variety of ways, for a range of specific purposes. The practice of gospel cooperation will depend upon the specific context in which Christians, churches or organizations seek to work together. Organizations such as FIEC, TGC and UCCF therefore take slightly different views on matters outside core gospel doctrines. FIEC is a family of churches with a distinct ecclesiology, so it rightly takes a particular position on women's ministry and holds that elders and pastors must be men. It does not, however, elevate this to the level of gospel requirement, and is willing to fellowship and co-operate in mission with those churches and individuals who take a different view on women's ministry. TGC takes a view not just on women's ministry, but also upholds a Reformed doctrine of soteriology, believing that this is important for the defence of the gospel in the US context.[49] UCCF exists to make disciples of Jesus Christ in the student world, by enabling students to work together in evangelism on campus and make the most of the unique opportunities of the university environment. It therefore does not take a position on either of these issues.

The New Testament makes clear that all true believers in the Lord Jesus are united in him.[50] They have been baptized into his one body by the one Spirit, and are brothers and sisters in him.[51] Christian unity is not something we are called to create, but rather something we are called to express. The imperative commands to unity in the New Testament flow from the indicative reality of our unity in Christ.

Christians express their unity with one another in local churches, which are assemblies of believers, and they in turn express their unity by relationships of fellowship with one another despite geographical distinction. Only in eternity will the whole body of Christ finally be gathered together before his throne.[52] Until that day the expression of our unity in Christ will only ever be preliminary and partial. The great task of the church is to go and make disciples of all nations by proclaiming the gospel,[53] and showcase to the world the new community of the eternal age to come.[54] Christians must work together to accomplish their gospel mission, which will require the sharing of resources of people and money so that the gospel can be spread among all people.[55]

Many churches join together in denominational structures that are defined not just by core gospel beliefs, but by common convictions on secondary issues such as baptism. Churches may cooperate with other like-minded gospel churches, whether informally or through more structured organizations that facilitate this, and such groupings vary as to the degree to which they are defined by secondary issues. It is increasingly common, for example, for local churches in a city or region to work together to advance the gospel in their area, whether by church growth or by church planting, across denominational lines because they hold common gospel convictions. As Christianity declines and the gospel need becomes more obvious,[56] secondary distinctives become less important in comparison with the overriding, great task of seeing lost people come to saving faith in the Lord Jesus. Gospel churches and individual Christians may also cooperate in pandenominational or parachurch organizations to advance the gospel.

The mere fact that churches and individuals hold essential gospel convictions in common does not mean that it will always be possible, necessary or wise to work together. Those who hold to core gospel convictions will still have a variety of different convictions on secondary matters, which remain important to them, and a diversity of cultural tastes and preferences. They may be seeking to reach very different communities or groups, which would require the gospel message and gospel ministry to be contextualized in mutually incompatible ways.

We should not assume that not cooperating in gospel ministry is always a failure. In many cases it may be essential to work separately so as to reach different communities and cultures. There is no one-size-fits-all gospel ministry, and much gospel cooperation is most effective between relatively homogeneous groups. The level of commonality required will depend upon the specific project being undertaken. For example, a broader group of evangelicals can cooperate to stand firm for the core truths of the gospel than can work together to plant a specific local church, where decisions about ecclesiology, church government, the sacraments, ministry and style will have to be taken, or to found a seminary or run a training course for ministry. A joint mission in a town or city will find it difficult to draw all gospel leaders to work together if some are adamant that supernatural healing ought to be an integral aspect of the outreach, while others believe strongly that it should not.

In the New Testament we discover that not everything was done cooperatively, but rather there was an overriding mutual respect and understanding that enabled the gospel to flourish in multiple communities. James, Peter and John took the gospel to the Jews, and established churches with a Jewish culture that showed a high regard for circumcision, the dietary laws, sabbaths and festivals, whereas Paul and Barnabas took the gospel to the Gentiles and planted multi-ethnic churches that did not observe the requirement of the law.[57] Paul and Barnabas eventually went their separate ways in ministry because they could not agree over the place of John Mark in their church-planting team.[58]

There will be times when our cultural preferences, personality differences, ministry callings and desire to advocate for secondary issues we consider important will prevent us from cooperating for every purpose. The proper response in such cases is to respect one another's differences and to bless one another in our respective gospel initiatives. We ought not to view each other as rivals, nor to undertake our ministry competitively, seeking to achieve greater 'market share' at one another's expense. For example, in large towns or cities there is usually ample scope for multiple churches reflecting different ecclesiologies, all of which can contribute to the work of the gospel in that community. In a smaller town that lacks a gospel witness, or that already has a gospel church but of a different kind, it would be missionally inappropriate to plant a new church to accommodate those with a secondary-issue preference

Gospel cooperation generally requires us to set aside our personal preferences and 'rights' for the sake of a greater ability to reach the lost for Christ. If local churches join together in a common mission to their town, or students join in a Christian Union to evangelize their campus, then complementarians and egalitarians may, for example, have to set aside their personal convictions for the sake of the greater good. This is exactly the approach that Paul adopted in his evangelistic ministry.[59] Egalitarians should therefore be willing to respect the consciences of their complementarian brothers and sisters and not insist on having a female preacher for a joint mission, and complementarians should refrain from judging their egalitarian brothers and sisters because they take a different view on women's ministry. Inevitably gospel cooperation will mean a willingness to compromise around that which is held in common, both doctrinally and culturally, and will require immense wisdom, grace and maturity.

Conclusions

Evangelicals have a long history of cooperating in the work of the gospel. Evangelicalism has always been a pandenominational movement, focused on convictions and practices that born-again believers have in common with each other, and that to some extent transcend their ecclesiological loyalties. Gospel cooperation has brought great blessings and has enabled the kingdom of God to grow more rapidly and more effectively than would otherwise have been the case.[60]

The gospel cooperation between Whitefield, Wesley and Edwards was a vital aspect of the Great Awakening that led to the rise of evangelicalism.[61] The establishment of non-denominational evangelical missionary societies greatly contributed to the cause of world evangelization. In the nineteenth century the holiness movement and prophecy conferences led to the establishment of events such as the Keswick Convention, which drew evangelicals together. In the 1920s evangelicals from different denominations worked together to produce *The Fundamentals* so as to protect the church from the onslaughts of liberal theology. The creation of the Inter-Varsity Fellowship, now UCCF, has enabled generations of students to work together to share the good news about the Lord Jesus on campus. The Revd E.J. Poole-Connor drew inspiration from such evangelical unity movements, especially Keswick and the mission societies, to establish FIEC in 1922 as a means of bringing independent evangelical churches together in 'a society of mutual helpfulness'.[62]

Cooperation in the gospel is not, however, merely a matter of pragmatic benefit. It helps to model the unity of the people of God in the body of Christ. For all its weaknesses and theological failings, the ecumenical movement was right to recognize that a lack of Christian unity is a barrier to mission. In the eyes of a watching world, church division undermines the truth and credibility of the Christian faith. Jesus prayed for the unity of his people,[63] and the apostles strove to achieve and maintain it.[64] While it is inevitable that there must be division between true and false believers, and between true and false churches, there can be no excuse for division between true gospel people and churches. As has been noted, this does not mean that they will always cooperate in their specific work, but it ought to mean that they do not work against each other, acting as if they are competitors fighting for market share.

Sadly, evangelicals sometimes fail to cooperate for reasons that are wholly unconnected with guarding the truth of the gospel. Clashes of culture, class, race, personality or rivalry can be obstacles to cooperation. Cooperation is prevented by ignorance or prejudice, or even the wilful refusal to think the best of others. Cooperation is rendered impossible where individuals are competing for leadership and influence, or when they are seeking to build a personal following or ministry. The disagreement between Lloyd-Jones and John Stott in 1966, with all the tragic consequences that followed, was in part a consequence of their very different temperaments, nationalities, class backgrounds, ministry styles, leadership expectations and ages.[65]

Perhaps the greatest threat to gospel cooperation comes from elevating issues of secondary importance, or even mere matters of style, to primary importance, thus rendering it impossible to work alongside those who hold a different view or who do things a different way. This is often the result of good intentions, as leaders are convinced that if everyone did things their way the gospel would advance more quickly. For example, some leaders might teach and act as if the problems of the church would be resolved if only everyone were to share their beliefs about baptism and church membership, whereas others might think that only their specific style of expository preaching is truly faithful to the text. It requires a large measure of grace and perspective to realize that many of the things we highly value are of only relatively minor importance to the advance of the gospel. One of the insights that motivated E.J. Poole-Connor to strive for evangelical cooperation, both within and beyond the FIEC, was that God had blessed all kinds of evangelical groups and ministries in times of revival, irrespective of their different views and their individual confidence that they were right.[66] Over the centuries the Lord had blessed evangelical Anglicans, Baptists, Congregationalists and Brethren, and seemed to have shown no favouritism between them because of their differences. He did not grant or withhold his blessing on the basis of their secondary beliefs.

The inability of evangelicals to cooperate, even when they are united in core gospel convictions, too often reflects an inability to accept that they cannot have everything exactly as they would wish. All too often we would rather establish a rival church, mission, training course, conference or ministry if we cannot have things done in exactly the way we believe best. Even if cooperating would mean that we gained 90% of what we wanted, we would rather start our own alternative to ensure that we can achieve the full 100%. If we want to pursue gospel cooperation without compromise we need not only to guard the gospel, but also our hearts against the temptation to work together only when we get everything our way. Cooperation within the 'gospel space' between non-negotiable primary doctrines and false teaching will always involve an element of compromise to serve the common good rather than to pursue our own interests.

The challenges facing the church in the West today have had the effect of fostering a greater gospel cooperation between evangelicals, in much the same way that persecution has done in the past. Core evangelical beliefs have been attacked from 'within the camp', which has driven those who hold tenaciously to them to stand together. The increasing realization that we are living in a missionary context has also caused evangelicals to prioritize reaching the lost rather than pursuing factional interest. As secularism advances, the challenges are likely to become even greater. Churches, congregants and ministers in denominations that approve or accept same-sex relationships will have to decide whether they can remain without compromising the gospel. Independents and those in denominations that are firmly evangelical will increasingly need to work together rather than pursue their own agenda. The dangers of compromise will be avoided, and cooperation that advances the gospel facilitated, only if we maintain gospel clarity and practise gospel generosity. Professor Carson has modelled both gospel clarity and gospel generosity to us. It remains for us to ensure that we continue to build on his example in the years to come.

Notes

1. Leicester: Inter-Varsity Press, 1991.
2. Grand Rapids, Mich.: Baker, 1987.
3. Leicester: Apollos, 1996.
4. Leicester: Inter-Varsity Press, 1991.
5. Leicester: Inter-Varsity Press, 1992.
6. Grand Rapids, Mich.: Baker, 1984.
7. Grand Rapids, Mich.: Baker, 2007.
8. <http://www.fiec.org.uk>. See also John Stevens (ed.), *Independent Church: Biblically Shaped and Gospel Driven* (Leyland: 10, 2014).
9. <http://www.thegospelcoalition.org>.
10. D.M. Lloyd-Jones, 'Evangelical Unity: An Appeal', in *Knowing the Times* (Edinburgh: Banner of Truth, 1989).
11. See Andrew Atherstone, 'Lloyd-Jones and the Anglican Secession Crisis', in Andrew Atherstone and Ceri Jones (eds.), *Engaging With Martyn Lloyd-Jones* (Nottingham: Apollos, 2011), pp. 261–292.
12. See, for example, Mark 1:14–15; Acts 2:22–39.
13. Thiselton, for example, argues that this phrase undoubtedly entails propitiation (Anthony C. Thiselton, *The First Epistle to the Corinthians* [Grand Rapids, Mich.: Eerdmans; Carlisle: Paternoster, 2000], p. 1191).
14. 1 Cor. 15:42–49.
15. See 1 Cor. 8:6; Rom. 1:4.
16. 1 Cor. 8:6.
17. Acts 2:14–41; 3:11–26; 7:1–53; 10:34–43; 13:16–41; 14:8–20; 17:16–34.
18. See, for example, Alan Mann and Steve Chalke, *The Lost Message of Jesus* (Grand Rapids, Mich.: Zondervan, 2004).

19. John Stott, *The Cross of Christ*, 2nd ed. (Leicester: Inter-Varsity Press,
     1989); Steve Jefferey, Mike Ovey and Andrew Sach, *Pierced for Our
     Transgressions: Rediscovering the Glory of Penal Substitution* (Nottingham:
     Inter-Varsity Press, 2007); Donald Macleod, *Christ Crucified:
     Understanding the Atonement* (Nottingham: Inter-Varsity Press, 2014).

20. It was for this reason that in 1910 the Cambridge University Inter-
     Collegiate Christian Union split with the Student Christian Movement.
     See Oliver Barclay and Robert Horn, *From Cambridge to the World:
     125 Years of Student Witness* (Leicester: Inter-Varsity Press, 2002).

21. Gal. 1:11–12; Rom. 1:1–6; Eph. 3:2–9.

22. 2 Peter 3:16.

23. See D.A. Carson (ed.), *The Enduring Authority of the Christian Scriptures*
     (Nottingham: Inter-Varsity Press, 2016).

24. <https://fiec.org.uk/about-us/beliefs>.

25. <https://www.thegospelcoalition.org/about/foundation-documents>.

26. <https://www.uccf.org.uk/about/doctrinal-basis.htm>.

27. See, for example, D.A. Carson and Timothy Keller, *The Gospel as Centre*
     (Wheaton, Ill.: Crossway, 2012).

28. See also Phillip Jensen, *The Limits of Fellowship, the Inclusiveness of Love*
     (Leyland: 10, 2012).

29. This is the practical outcome of 'handing them over to Satan', which
     means that they are symbolically removed from the kingdom of God and
     returned to the kingdom of Satan. See 1 Tim. 1:18–20; 1 Cor. 5:4–5, 9–11.

30. 1 Tim. 1:18–19.

31. Cf. Titus 1:13; 2:1.

32. 1 John 2:22.

33. 2 John 7.

34. 1 Cor. 15:12–19; 2 Tim. 2:18; Titus 1:10–16; 3:9–11.

35. 2 Peter 3:3–7.

36. Gal. 4:8–11; Phil. 3:2; Col. 2:16–23.

37. 1 Tim. 4:1–5.

38. 1 Cor. 5:1–5; 6:12–20; 2 Peter 2; Jude; Rev. 2:20–23.

39. 1 Tim. 6:1–5.

40. Rom. 14:5.

41. Rom. 14:1 – 15:13; 1 Cor. 10:23–33.

42. See John Stevens, 'The Pastor and Gospel Partnership', in Steve
     Timmis and Melvin Tinker (eds.), *The Renewed Pastor* (Fearn: Mentor,
     2011), pp. 261–292.

43. <https://fiec.org.uk/resources/article/gospel-unity-statement>.

44. Acts 15:29; Rom. 1:24–27; 1 Cor. 6:18–20; 2 Cor. 12:21; Gal. 5:19; Eph. 4:3; Col. 3:5; 1 Thess. 4:3–8; Heb. 13:4; 1 Peter 4:3.

45. For an assessment of contemporary Roman Catholicism see Gregg Allison, *Roman Catholic Theology and Practice* (Wheaton, Ill.: Crossway, 2014).

46. For examples of self-identifying 'evangelicals' who advocate the acceptance of same-sex relationships see Alan Wilson, *More Perfect Union: Understanding Same-Sex Marriage* (London: DLT, 2014); Matthew Vines, *God and the Gay Christian* (New York: Convergent, 2014); Jane Ozanne (ed.), *Journeys in Grace and Truth: Revisiting Scripture and Sexuality* (London: Ekklesia, 2016).

47. Matt. 7:21–23.

48. See especially Jonathan Leeman, *The Church and the Surprising Offence of God's Love* (Wheaton, Ill.: Crossway, 2009).

49. <https://www.thegospelcoalition.org/about/foundation-documents>.

50. John 17:20–23.

51. Eph. 4:4–6; Phil. 2:1–4.

52. Rev. 7:1–10.

53. Matt. 28:16–20.

54. John 13:34–35; 17:23; Eph. 3:10–11.

55. As, for example, in Acts 11:27–30; Rom. 15:24; 2 Cor. 8:1 – 9:15; Phil. 1:5; 4:14–16.

56. It is estimated that no more than 3% of the UK population are genuine born-again believers in the Lord Jesus, and the growth rate of evangelicalism in the UK in 2012 was 0%. See Jason Mandryk, *Operation World*, 7th ed. (Downers Grove, Ill.: InterVarsity Press, 2012), for more information.

57. Gal. 2:9.

58. Acts 15:36–41.

59. 1 Cor. 9:19–23.

60. See also Chris Bruno and Matt Dirks, *Churches Partnering Together: Biblical Strategies for Fellowship, Evangelism and Compassion* (Wheaton, Ill.: Crossway, 2014).

61. See Mark Noll, *The Rise of Evangelicalism* (Nottingham: Inter-Varsity Press, 2011).

62. *Evangelical Unity* (FIEC, 1941), pp. 174–188.

63. John 17:21.

64. Eph. 4:3–6.
65. See Gaius Davies, *Genius Grief and Grace* (Fearn: Christian Focus, 2008); Alister Chapman, *Godly Ambition: John Stott and the Evangelical Movement* (Oxford: Oxford University Press, 2014).
66. *Evangelical Unity.*

7. THE SILENCE OF GOD

William Edgar

The defeat of France by the Nazi forces in June of 1940 was remarkable for its speed and decisiveness. After wrongly anticipating an attack across the eastern border, the French were caught off guard when the Germans came down through the Ardennes and met the poorly prepared French forces with brutal finality. Many reasons have been adduced for the nearly sudden collapse.[1] Among them are the weakened position of France's Third Republic following the First World War, increasing doubts about French resilience, the failure to anticipate Hitler's surprise move through neutral Holland and Belgium, and the overly complicated bureaucracy among the Allies. The entire conquest took only six weeks. Two million Parisians fled south, including president Albert Lebrun, who wondered what the miscellaneous French troops he observed on the way were doing, sitting idle in the villages and countryside. Hitler, bent on revenge, humiliated France by forcing them to sign the armistice on 22 June 1940 in the very same railway carriage in the forest of Compiègne that had been the site of the German surrender after World War I in 1918.[2]

France was forcibly divided into two zones, the occupied North and the so-called Free South, led by a former war hero, 84-year-old

Maréchal Henri Philippe Pétain, in Vichy. For five long years France suffered the cruel presence of the German forces.[3] At first, many French people simply complied and resigned themselves to the occupation. A few did resist. We may never know the extent of the French resistance, as numerous people after the war claimed to have been a part of it, in numbers that would defy credibility.[4] There may have been tens of thousands in the early years, and up to several hundred thousand by the last years of the war.[5] A few deeply moving cases of harbouring Jews from certain deportation could be found. They were the exception. Perhaps the most familiar example is from the Plateau Ardéchois, where several small farming villages, populated mostly by Huguenot Christians, were able to provide a haven for a few thousand Jews, many of them children.[6] But again, this was by far the exception.

Vercors

One of the most revealing windows into the France of the occupation is some of the literature written clandestinely during that time. Though not necessarily written by believing Christians, many reflections on the problem of evil and the apparent silence of God were composed. Albert Camus wrote most of his masterpiece *La Peste* (*The Plague*) from a small flat in Le Chambon.[7] The villagers remember his being there but do not seem to know many details about his stay. Camus's novel involves several levels. The first is the fictional account of the bubonic plague coming to the Algerian town of Oran. Camus masterfully chronicles the coming of this horrible pandemic to the unsuspecting townspeople, with all of the psychological reactions and intrigue being detailed by this master novelist. At a deeper level it is impossible to miss the allusion to, if not the metaphor of, the Nazi occupation. One striking analogy between the story and the surrounding occupation is Camus's highlighting of the comparison between two comportments: resistance or collaboration. Several of the characters in Camus's story denied the plague until they could not avoid it. Others fought it with the means at hand. Clearly one of the main characters in the story, Doctor Rieux, is modelled after the village doctor in Le Chambon, Roger Le Forestier, who gave himself selflessly to the cause of protecting the refugees. The priest, Father Paneloux, is a complex figure, much as was André Trocmé, pastor of the Reformed Church in Le Chambon, although in a very different way. Early on, Paneloux preached a sermon in which he basically blamed the people for the judgment of the plague. He later softened his views considerably. The third level of the novel is about *theodicy*, or the problem of evil. Why the plague? Why the affliction of this particular town? Where is God?

The most powerful text from this time is, without a doubt, *Le Silence de la Mer* by Vercors. The short story is fictional, though starkly realistic. A German officer, Werner von Ebrennac, quarters in the modest home of a man and his niece. The lieutenant is cultured, a considerable musician, an admirer of French literature. Every evening he enters the house and holds forth on the glories of French literature, a subject on which he is an expert. Molière, Racine, Hugo, Voltaire, Rabelais, these are like a crowd entering the theatre: 'We don't know whom to let in first.' He also loves German music, and feels it is better than French music. His hope is that the two countries can one day unite and pool their traditions. He wants the superiority of French literature to become allied with the genius of German music.

But every night he is met by the complete silence of his two French hosts. He then retires to his bedroom saying simply, 'Je vous souhaite une bonne nuit' (I wish you a good night). In the end von Ebrennac is called to Paris and learns of his dreadful duty, not creating an alliance, but generating further oppression. The reader somehow feels for the man, even though he is clearly the enemy. The story is beautifully told, and, like *La Peste*, carries many levels. The book was mostly extremely well received. It was made into a film noir in 1949, directed by the brilliant Jean-Pierre Melville (his real name was Jean-Pierre Grumbach, but he so admired the American author Herman Melville that he changed his name). The story has been translated into many languages. The best English version is by Cyril Connolly.[8]

Le Silence de la Mer was published clandestinely in Paris, and only the editor, Pierre de Lescure, knew the true identity of its author, whose real name was Jean Bruller (1902–91). Bruller was mobilized in 1939 but was soon wounded in the knee and able to retire to the family home in Villiers-sur-Morin (1940), near a real place called

Vercors, where he wrote the novel. It was the first of several texts published by the newly founded Éditions de Minuit, the foremost French underground resistance press. Bruller's father was Hungarian, his mother from the French province of Berry. Though a member of the Communist Party, he resigned after the Soviet repression of Hungary. Just before his death he told the magazine *Globe*, 'What interested me right after the war, with Nazism, is the definition of what truly is man, what is human about humanity.'[9]

The library in the story represents not only a piece of furniture, but a fourth character. Its books are eloquent. Von Ebrennac loves to study the titles, caressing the bindings, and often makes comments on the books. His remarks are nevertheless met with complete silence. It could be that he admired the attitude of his hosts, whose silence represents the grandeur and dignity of their high civilization. When the officer finds out the dreadful designs of his fellow Nazis he deeply laments the hypocrisy of their refusal to allow French books to be made available, with the exception of certain technical manuals. Not only are Péguy, Proust and Bergson forbidden, but also the most recent literature. In an obvious allusion to the German *auto da Fé* of 1933 he remarks that the occupiers will ironically extinguish the flame and thus darken the light that once came from Europe. The library is the symbolic remnant which Les Éditions de Minuit were meant to save and foster.

There is some ambivalence in the way Vercors renders the silence of the uncle and his niece. On the one hand, the silence is one of politeness, one of cordiality, which is understood, perhaps even welcomed, by the officer. As we mentioned, the civilized German probably recognizes the dignity of the French attitude. On the other hand, there is no doubt a silence of condemnation, a sort of sentence pronounced without words, a posture of resistance against the oppressor. It is of considerable interest that not everyone reacted positively to this story. Arthur Koestler, for example, did not approve of the character of von Ebrennac, because he wondered how this man could have ignored the intentions of his countrymen for so long. He further reproached Vercors for having the uncle and niece so severely judge a man who was, if not anti-Nazi, a critic of the Nazi policies.[10] Communists in Algeria even suspected Vercors of collaboration, since his character is so sympathetic. They rather missed the true nature of the drama. To defend himself Vercors felt he should explain his choices. The officer was actually modelled on Ernst Jünger, who lived an astonishingly long life (1895–1998), and was a cultured anarchist whose journals recount a level of war deeper than the surface conflict between countries.[11] At some levels attractive, he was nevertheless a turncoat.

Whence the Silence of God?

Does Vercors have a religious concern? Perhaps not overtly, and yet it is difficult to avoid some kind of association with the theodicy question. Why the occupation? Where is God in the midst of the suffering? Silence here refers not only to the man and his niece, but to the world in its turmoil. Where is the meaning? Why does not a clear voice ring out and guide the victims through their plight?

The theme of silence as it relates to the presence of God often appears in literary and musical works. One of the most commanding in the post-war years is the novel *Silence* by Japanese author Shusaku Endo.[12] The setting is seventeenth-century Japan, in a period when, having initially accepted the Christian faith through Francis Xavier, the country has now outlawed it. Many inroads had been made and a good many Japanese people had become Christians. But then persecution set in and became increasingly cruel. The climax of the story comes when the protagonist, the missionary Father Sebastian Rodrigues, is betrayed by the Judas-like character Kichijiro for a few small silver coins. Threatened with torture and with the murder of many Christians, and having learned that his own mentor Fereira has apostatized, Rodrigues is pressured into stamping on a *fumie*, an image of Christ on the cross. He succumbs and then becomes a part of the establishment. Disgraced by the church, he nevertheless remains secretly a follower of Christ, who, after all, had died for those who betrayed him. Throughout, Rodrigues and others are puzzled by the apparent silence of Christ during the time of missionary activity for his sake. Yet the last words of the novel are these: 'Our Lord was not silent. Even if he had been silent, my life to this day would have spoken of him.' What can this mean?

The theme of God's silence can be found in both popular and more classical music. The lyrics often reflect on the lack of meaning in the world, or on the apparent absence of answered prayer. Consider the recent piece by folk singer Andrew Peterson:

It's enough to drive a man crazy; it'll break a man's faith
It's enough to make him wonder if he's ever been sane
When he's bleating for comfort from Thy staff and Thy rod
And the heaven's only answer is the silence of God

It'll shake a man's timbers when he loses his heart
When he has to remember what broke him apart
This yoke may be easy, but this burden is not
When the crying fields are frozen by the silence of God

And if a man has got to listen to the voices of the mob
Who are reeling in the throes of all the happiness they've got
When they tell you all their troubles have been nailed up to that cross
Then what about the times when even followers get lost?
'Cause we all get lost sometimes . . .

There's a statue of Jesus on a monastery knoll
In the hills of Kentucky, all quiet and cold
And He's kneeling in the garden, as silent as a Stone
All His friends are sleeping and He's weeping all alone

And the man of all sorrows, he never forgot
What sorrow is carried by the hearts that he bought
So when the questions dissolve into the silence of God
The aching may remain, but the breaking does not
The aching may remain, but the breaking does not
In the holy, lonesome echo of the silence of God[13]

Silence can be represented in lyrics in several ways. The most obvious is the one just cited, where the silence of God as experienced in life is simply declaimed. It is a mystery, a suffering to be endured. But it can also be more positive, commending a proper sense of awe before the Almighty. Johann Sebastian Bach several times alluded to this kind of silence in his cantatas and passions. For example, in Cantata 128, *Auf Christi Himmelfahrt allein* (*On Christ's ascent to Heaven Alone*), the second aria declares that though he is ascended, yet 'Sein Allmacht zu ergründen, wird kein Mensch finden' (His omnipotence will no person discover). The recitative leading up to this was originally 'So schweig, verwegnen Mund, und suche nicht dieselbe zu ergründen!' (So be silent, presumptuous mouth, and do not attempt to fathom this). Commenting on this, Eric Chafe compares this silence to another cantata, and states, 'In Cantata 87 the idea of silence expresses both intimate contact with God (who knows the unspoken heart of the believer) and the patient enduring of worldly tribulation.'[14]

Another, related way silence may be represented in music is that the composition can transport the participant into the presence of God, which requires a proper silence, or at least a quietness conducive to worship. In some cases the musical material can become, as it were, iconic. The eccentric British composer John Tavener reflects on this longing for God in his *The Music of Silence*. He tells us he has attempted to 'produce that kind of ecstatic frozen petrified silence [captured by the great icons from the Byzantine period] in music.' He adds that this kind of silence cannot be the absence of sound, since proper music should contain implicit silence.[15] Tavener draws on the traditions from before the Renaissance for his music, a culture he finds less rationalistic, and thus, for him, more favourable to contemplation.[16]

Silence in Scripture

Our age is full of chatter. Words blare out at us from every corner. The noise has driven some people to escape into a life of relative silence. Yet escape is not the best posture for believers. Instead, we place our hope in the God who has spoken, whose will cannot be properly known apart from the corrective, clarifying role of verbal revelation. This is a subject which has preoccupied D.A. Carson, to whom these meditations are lovingly dedicated, throughout his academic life.[17] This hope should lead us, not away from the world, but into the world where we may seek to do it good.

Perhaps surprisingly, the Bible, which is the principal repository of this Word from God, contains considerable insights on silence. Its wisdom tells us there is 'a time to keep silence, and a time to speak' (Eccl. 3:7).[18] One of the appropriate occasions for being silent is during evil times. This approach parallels what we saw from Vercors. Consider Amos 5:13: 'Therefore he who is prudent will keep silent in such a time, for it is an evil time.' The prophet is no doubt addressing the type of chatter that characterized his own culture, where babble and noise were a cover-up for the crimes of the people. Instead, by doing good, we may 'put to silence the ignorance of foolish people' (1 Peter 2:15). And, for that matter, 'Even a fool who keeps silent is considered wise; when he closes his lips, he is deemed intelligent' (Prov. 17:28). I have often regretted speaking out about some matter. I have almost never regretted staying quiet. Once I did have an opportunity to defend the gospel, and I did not, not because I was ashamed of it, but because I did not want to begin an argument. I should have done so. But I have usually been glad to have kept silence.

Conversely, there are times to refrain from silence. Carrying one's guilt unconfessed becomes destructive of our very bodies. King David admits, 'For when I kept silent, my bones wasted away through my groaning all day long.' The reason? As he puts it, 'For day and night your hand was heavy upon me; my strength was dried up as by the heat of summer' (Ps. 32:3–4). No doubt the most urgent occasion for not keeping silence is when it is our duty to enlighten others about God's requirements. We remember the dreadful words to Ezekiel, wherein the Lord tells him he is a watchman for his kindred. If the watchman fails to warn his brethren of God's judgment, then their blood is on his hands (Ezek. 33:7–9). To be sure, the trumpet does need to be clear. The same applies to the need for intelligible worship. If a congregant speaks only the sounds of glossolalia, then the bugle is giving an indistinct sound, says Paul, and so the assembly is not properly edified (1 Cor. 14:7–12). But if there is no interpretation, then silence is enjoined (1 Cor. 14:28).

Guilty silence is not golden. Think of the psalmist's hesitation, followed by his decision to address his neighbour about his shortcomings: 'These [sinful] things you have done, and I have been silent . . . But now I rebuke you and lay the charge before you' (Ps. 50:21). So, then, there is an appropriate time to be vocal, when we can help our fellow human. The New Testament letters address the matter. We must never speak evil against a brother (Jas 4:11–12). Yet we are duty-bound to confess our sins to one another, and even to bring back 'a sinner from his wandering' (Jas 5:16, 19–20). We should bear one another's burdens and seek to restore anyone caught in transgression (Gal. 6:1–2; cf. Ps. 141:5).

The Grace of Christ's Silence

If for us there is 'a time to keep silence, and a time to speak', is that not also true for God himself? There could be no worse famine than the famine of the Word of God (Amos 8:11). The absence of a true prophet is a worse curse than the absence of any other kind of information (Ps. 74:9). This has to be true, even though we know of times and occasions where the dearth of information has been devastating. Think of times of war, or oppressive regimes where not only may there not be information, but also what there is may be politically manipulated. Still, better this kind of disinformation than a famine of God's Word. And so, how well we can appreciate the 'good news', the fact that *He Is There and He Is Not Silent*.[19]

Having said this, are there not occasions when God's silence is salutary? We are immediately drawn to the compelling accounts of Jesus' suffering and sacrifice. Isaiah 53:7 predicts,

> He was oppressed, and he was afflicted,
>   yet he opened not his mouth;
> like a lamb that is led to the slaughter,
>   and like a sheep that before its shearers is silent,
>   so he opened not his mouth.

Commenting on this prophecy, J. Ridderbos says, '[The Servant of the Lord] will Himself be humiliated without offering resistance, even without "opening his mouth" to resist verbally or to pay back in kind the words of abuse aimed at Him (cf. 1 Pet. 2:23).'[20] This silence of the sacrificial lamb is recognized throughout the Scriptures as the main image for the centrepiece of Jesus' finished work on the cross. It was this very passage from Isaiah that puzzled the Ethiopian eunuch returning from Jerusalem and that Philip was able to explain to him (Acts 8:26–40). Jesus' humiliation, represented as the sacrificial lamb, is the gateway to salvation for God's people. The apostle

John underscores the propitiatory nature of Christ's work from the very first, when he records John the Baptist's declaration 'Behold, the Lamb of God, who takes away the sin of the world!' (John 1:29, 36; cf. Exod. 12:3; 1 Peter 1:19). In Revelation, Christ is called the Lamb who was slain (5:12; 13:8).

Christ's silence will take on a literal expression during his trial. When Pilate asks him, 'Where are you from?', he gives no answer (John 19:9). In Mark's version the high priest and Pilate challenge him to give answers to the many accusations brought against him (Mark 14:60; 15:4; cf. Matt. 26:62). According to Mark 15:5 he makes no further answer, 'so that Pilate was amazed'. Some of the ancient commentators discern the dynamics going on. Ephrem the Syrian notes that while others gain victory through making defences, 'our Lord gained victory through his silence, because the recompense of his death through divine silence was the victory of true teaching . . . He kept silent so that his silence would make [his calumniators] even louder, and so that his crown would be made more beautiful through all this clamor.'[21] John Calvin, commenting on Matthew 26:62–63, says, 'Christ was again silent, not only because the objection was frivolous, but because, having been appointed to be a sacrifice, he had thrown aside all anxiety about defending himself.'[22] Carson astutely remarks that Jesus' silence is not absolute, since he would speak again. But, he asks, 'What answer, long or brief, could Jesus have provided for the Roman prefect who is more interested in political manoeuvring than in justice . . . ?'[23]

The Most Dreadful Silence of All

If Jesus' silence is explained by his obedient intention to submit to the trial that would lead to his death, there is a more terrible silence still. It is, of course, the silence of the Father towards his only begotten Son during the dreadful hours of his final sacrifice. Two moments of extreme torment can be singled out. The first is when Jesus prayed in the Garden of Gethsemane. Knowing the terrible destiny that he needed to face, his soul was full of sorrow and trouble, a sorrow unto death (Matt. 26:37–38; Mark 14:33–34). Three times he prayed for this cup of God's wrath to be taken away from him. But it could not be. The disciples fell into a strange sleep, leaving him all alone. He sweated drops of blood, knowing what he must endure (Luke 22:44). No word from the Father is recorded, although an angel did appear to give him strength (Luke 22:43). Jesus, of course, after his plea, says, 'nevertheless, not as I will, but as you will' (Matt. 26:39).

We tend to see Jesus Christ as so characteristically divine that his humanity is secondary. Nothing could be farther from the truth. In the felicitous Chalcedonian formulation, he was one person, but in two natures. His human nature was not secondary but integral to his one person. With respect to his humanity, the Son of God was subject to such emotions as sorrow and the fear of death. Jesus is no Socrates, nor is he a Buddha. He is indeed God, but is God in the flesh. So, when he says, 'not as I will,' he means that if he could have his way as a human being, he would not choose to go through the agonizing torture that awaited him. But he knew at the deepest level that he could not have his way in this. Rather, what he truly desired was to do the will of the Father. These are deep mysteries. We have no real idea of what Jesus was going through. He was contemplating the most dreadful moment in all of history, being separated from the Father, whose wrath would be visited upon him in full measure. We must strenuously avoid trivializing this moment by referring to 'my cross to bear' and the like. Our Lord was about to experience the visitation of the Father's full anger against sin, not his, but ours. This is unique, never to be repeated.

The second moment of torment is when Jesus is hanging on the cross. This instrument of terror was devised by the Romans in order to shame the victim while he was dying. It is among the most agonizing forms of torture ever designed. On it the innocent Jesus was accursed, and became sin for us (Gal. 3:13; 2 Cor. 5:21). We must never imagine that somehow he was sent reluctantly by an abusive Father. The Father and Son had agreed from all eternity that this sacrifice was the only way to reconcile sinners to God (Ps. 40:7–8 ; Heb. 7:22). But yet at the climax of his suffering, he asks, with the psalmist, 'My God, my God, why have you forsaken me?' (Matt. 27:46; see Ps. 22:1). John Murray calls this 'the most mysterious utterance that ever ascended from earth to heaven'.[24] No answer is given. The Father has indeed abandoned the Son. He has delivered him up, so that we could be forgiven (Rom. 8:32).

But wait, how could this be? How can we reconcile God's silence with his love for his Son? Wonderfully, it is precisely here that love and justice meet. The opposite of love is not wrath but hate. The Father was fully angry against the Son, who bore our iniquities on the tree, but without hating him. The Father's abandonment had a design: the redemption of his people. Mysteriously enough, this abandonment was the deepest expression of his inextinguishable love. At the very moment of the Father's silence against his beloved Son, he was still the eternal Father, who could never stop loving his begotten one. And by his abandoning his Son, the guilt and sin of his people was gone, finished, vanquished for ever. We must never forget that, however inscrutable, the moment when God was silent was also the moment when he could open his mouth to his people for ever.

Conclusion

Who is sufficient for these things? Not one of us. But they do drive us to contemplate the love of God for us, his people. Jesus did pray that the cup could be removed. It was not. But yet his prayers were heard: 'In the days of his flesh, Jesus offered up prayers and supplications, with loud cries and tears, to him who was able to save him from death, and he was heard because of his reverence' (Heb. 5:7). He was saved from the ultimate consequences of death: eternal perdition. He was not saved from death itself. It was this extraordinary insight that led Martin Luther to believe in the gospel. If Christ experienced the silence of God as described in Psalm 22, then salvation must be a gift, and not the result of spiritual discipline.

What Vercors understood about resistance was far better understood by the loving Father, whose Son was silent before his tormentors, and who was himself silent before his suffering Son, for our sake. The Nazi oppression of France and much of Europe was dreadful in its extent and depth. But it was a pale shadow of the oppression wrought by of human sinfulness. If the courageous remedy against the Nazis was the dignified silence of the man and his niece, the greater remedy for sin was the silence of God at the moment of Christ's greatest agony. The former led to the liberation of a marvellously civilized country from its oppressors. The latter, to the emancipation of sinners from the wrath of their holy God, and their safe harbour in his loving bosom for ever.

Notes

1. William L. Shirer's *The Collapse of the Third Republic: An Inquiry into the Fall of France in 1940* (New York: Simon & Schuster, 1969, 2014) remains the definitive analysis of the defeat.

2. Extraordinary film footage of this event is available from Journeyman Pictures <https://www.youtube.com/watch?v=vr4zJS4eb80>.

3. Many general histories exist. Among the most informative are Mark Bergère, *Une société en épuration* (Rennes: PUR, 2004); Yves Durand, *La France dans la Seconde Guerre Mondiale 1939–1945* (Paris: Armand Colin, 1989); Stanley Hoffmann, 'Le trauma de 1940', in J.-P. Azema and F. Bedarida (eds.), *La France des années noires* (Paris: Seuil, 1993), vol. 1, pp. 131–150.

4. Tilar J. Mazzeo, who wrote the fascinating *The Hotel on Place Vendôme*, was told by an elderly French woman, 'Most of those who tell you they were in the resistance are fabulists at best. The worst are simply liars. It was a frighteningly small movement, covert, secret, and the price of discovery was monstrous. After the war, everyone wanted to believe that they had supported it. It is a collective French national fantasy' (New York: HarperCollins, 2014), p. 4. This judgement may be too severe, but the facts are difficult to establish. See Jean-Marie Guirand and Pierre Laborie (eds.), *Mémoire et histoire de la Résistance* (Toulouse: Privat, 1995).

5. Claude Bourdet, *L'aventure incertaine* (Paris: Stock, 1975).

6. This number has been contested by some, who believe the actual figure is higher. Caroline Moorehead has given us a thorough account of the courageous activities in these villages, in which she deals with the statistics: *Village of Secrets: Defying the Nazis in Vichy France* (New York: HarperCollins, 2014), p. 336. A powerful documentary, *Weapons of the Spirit*, by filmmaker Pierre Sauvage, who was born in Le Chambon-sur-Lignon during the occupation, records the people and places where these events occurred.

7. Camus was a true participant in the resistance. Michel Onfray has recently written a defence of Camus's authenticity and compares him

      to Jean-Paul Sartre, who preached resistance but never really practised it. *L'ordre libertaire: La vie philosophique d'Albert Camus* (Paris: Éditions 84, 2013).

8. *The Silence of the Sea* (New York: Macmillan, 1944).

9. <http://www.terresdecrivains.com/vercors>.

10. See, Kevin De Ornellas, 'Macbeth, not Henry V: Shakespearean Allegory in the Construction of Vercors' "Good German"', in Pól Ó Dochartaign and Christiane Schönfeld (eds.), *Representing the 'Good German' in Literature and Culture After 1945: Altruism & Moral Ambiguity* (Rochester, N.Y.: Camden House, 2013), p. 185.

11. In a second edition of *Le Silence de la Mer* (1951), Vercors has the officer join the Eastern front in an act of suicidal submission. Even the best of Germans ends up compliant and for that should be condemned.

12. Shusaku Endo, *Silence (A Novel)* (Miami, Fla.: Taplinger, 1980). The book has also been made into a film by Martin Scorcese. A powerful study of the novel, in the setting of Japanese aesthetics, is by Makoto Fujimura, *Silence and Beauty* (Downers Grove, Ill.: InterVarsity Press, 2016).

13. <https://www.youtube.com/watch?v=cvytewIxllo>.

14. Eric Chafe, *J.S. Bach's Johannine Theology: The St John Passion and the Cantatas for Spring 1725* (New York: Oxford University Press, 2014), p. 476.

15. John Tavener, *The Music of Silence: A Composer's Testament*, ed. Brian Keeble (London: Faber & Faber, 1999), p. 157.

16. A Protestant response to this kind of spirituality would plead for a profound harmony between the verbal and the non-verbal, cautioning at once against rationalistic religion and irrationalist mysticism.

17. Consider only some of the most recent volumes he has either written or edited: *The Enduring Authority of the Christian Scriptures* (Grand Rapids, Mich.: Eerdmans, 2016); *NIV Zondervan Study Bible* (Grand Rapids, Mich.: Zondervan, 2015); *The Scriptures Testify About Me* (Wheaton, Ill.: Crossway, 2013); *Collected Writings on Scripture* (Wheaton, Ill.: Crossway, 2010); *Scripture and Truth* (Grand Rapids, Mich.: Baker, 1992).

18. Bible quotations in this chapter are from the English Standard Version.

19. The title of a key work by Francis A. Schaeffer (Wheaton, Ill.: Tyndale, 1973).

20. Jan Ridderbos, *Isaiah*, trans. John Vriend (Grand Rapids, Mich.: Zondervan/Regency, 1985), p. 480.

21. Quoted in Thomas C. Oden and Christopher A. Hall (eds.), *Ancient Christian Commentary on Scripture: New Testament II: Mark* (Downers Grove, Ill.: InterVarsity Press, 1998), p. 223.

22. John Calvin, *Commentaries*, vol. 33, trans. John King <http://www.sacred-texts.com/chr/calvin/cc33/cc33035.htm>.

23. D.A. Carson, *The Gospel According to John*, Pillar New Testament Commentaries (Leicester: Apollos; Grand Rapids, Mich.: Eerdmans, 1991), p. 600.

24. John Murray, *Redemption Accomplished and Applied* (Grand Rapids, Mich.: Eerdmans, 1955), p. 77.

Part III

8. WINNING HEARTS AND MINDS IN A SECULAR AGE

Richard M. Cunningham

Not so long ago, I was discussing a minor theological point with a friend who was trying to persuade me towards his view. When I pushed back against his position, he put on a North American accent and said in mock exasperation, 'Richard, I, I, I, I want to deconstruct your flawed hermeneutic and demonstrate that you are wrong for the following fifteen reasons . . .'

Why did I immediately recognize in that cheeky impersonation the voice of D.A. Carson?

For starters it was focused, uncompromising and (if he really had fifteen reasons) potentially persuasive. It matters little where you freeze frame a Don Carson sermon or highlight a section of a Carson book: wherever you dip in you observe a persuader at work.

Whether Carson is critiquing literary deconstruction in *The Gagging of God*[1] or speaking simply yet profoundly to the question of suffering in *How Long, O Lord?*,[2] readers find themselves confronted and engaged by a serious-minded, sympathetic (albeit unsentimental) persuader. Don does not write and speak with the air of one who vaguely hopes to communicate the veracity of his position. Rather, he marshals his ideas and arguments carefully so that no stone is left unturned, leaving his audience in little doubt as to where the truth lies.

Identification

In order to get close enough to an audience, to persuade them to change their mind, an effective communicator will work hard at identification. That is, to understand the mental landscape of his hearers and to articulate sympathetically the difficulties they have with what they are hearing, in such a way that they feel properly understood rather than caricatured or dismissed.

Epistemic humility and empathy have recently become much rarer commodities. This is especially true of our universities, which are at the sharp end of a more general cultural phenomenon: positions are becoming ever more polarized and the public space less civil and conducive to a proper debate about religion, sexual ethics and politics.

The dominance of identity politics has made the discussion of sensitive subjects difficult, if not impossible, for those who do not wish to be labelled with demeaning epithets.

You will be branded homophobic for not agreeing with gay marriage; sexist if you dare to put on separate men's and women's events;[3] Islamophobic if you suggest there could possibly be any link between Islam and violence towards Christians and Jews; transphobic if (like Peter Tatchell and Germaine Greer) you encourage open debate on transgender issues.[4]

Christian Union (CU) mission events have occasionally been threatened with cancellation by Student Unions (SUs) for potentially causing distress to the lesbian, gay, bisexual and transgender (LGBT) community as a result of 'harmful' or 'hateful' speech.

Safety: the Ultimate Good?

Those responses seem to emerge from a mindset in which 'safety' is the greatest good, whereas freedom of speech is a threat to that greater good since such freedom creates a risk of vulnerable students being harmed. The phenomena of 'safe spaces', 'trigger warnings' and 'protected characteristics' are now part of the university landscape, so much so that anyone speaking 'insensitively' is liable to receive complaints and sanctions.

Social media is able to whip up a massive reaction, which puts huge pressure on university authorities to yield to their fee-paying customers' demands. There does however seem to be a growing weariness with the fabricated outrage of click activists, resentment from some students at having certain newspapers banned, and growing cynicism at the plethora of demands being made on behalf of transgendered people.[5]

Nevertheless, I suspect things must probably get worse before universities get fed up with being bullied and made to take down statues, issue trigger warnings and being asked to build expensive new toilet facilities.

> Even universities, which are supposed to foster knowledge-sharing
> and spirited debate, are now suppressing it, for example by spinelessly
> rescinding speaking invitations to almost anyone that some group
> or another considers objectionable. When we fail to engage in such
> debates – when people choose 'safe spaces' over tough discussions –
> we lose our best chance of building consensus on how to solve at least
> some of our societies' pressing problems.[6]

False Moves

One easy false move we could make that will incline us to be shrill and defensive rather than engaging in our response is to see all this as primarily an anti-Christian mood. While university CUs are (collectively) the most vulnerable to accusations of hate speech on LGBT-related issues, the lust for 'safety' spares no one, not even the great progressive heroes and heroines of the past such as Greer and Tatchell.

Another false move would be to caricature all students as 'Generation Snowflake'.[7] We will cut off students' ears if we merely caricature what does seem to be an overprotected generation and one that has less appetite for robust exchanges of views. If we are to come close enough to win hearts and minds, we must understand that this generation of students is genuinely concerned not to cause distress and discomfort (unless on social media, where different rules seem to apply).

Generation Z is not used to robust engagement and heated debate and has experienced overprotective 'helicopter' parenting from Gen X parents, modelling for them the notion that the greatest good that can be conferred on another human is protection from harm. Libertarian and Christian pleas to safeguard freedom of speech, conscience and association seem too lofty and impersonal to connect with a generation that takes for granted those basic freedoms. And yet, as Benjamin Franklin observed, 'Those who would give up essential liberty to purchase a little temporary safety deserve neither freedom nor safety.'[8]

If we are to be heard by a generation that prizes safety above free speech, we must work hard at grasping the immensity of our task and realize that for all sorts of reasons (including the use of selective Facebook and other social media feeds) there is more tribal and less common ground than ever. If we are to be salt and light in society and challenge the chilling of public discourse in the name of 'safety', we must find ways to speak prophetically and engagingly into all this. But first we have to be close enough, in terms of identification, to be heard.

The secular challenges and objections to Christian faith seem to be growing in number and intensity, which makes the evangelistic task much harder. The average person in the UK not only regards Christianity as outmoded and unscientific but also as something that is deeply regressive and intolerant in its absolute truth claims. The student radicals of the 1960s have been dominating the political and cultural landscape for over a generation and have been selectively airbrushing Christian thought and Christian categories from public life.

As a result, the church's ability to engage with – let alone persuade – our secular society has rapidly diminished over the past few decades. The 2013 legal redefinition of marriage in England and Wales was a watershed moment and the clearest indication yet that our secular society regards biblical teaching as not merely antiquated but also profoundly regressive and intolerant. Christians who are convinced that the gospel is good news and the basis for ultimate human flourishing clearly have a task on their hands to get close enough to win hearts and minds.

Pacifism not Persuasion

There is a reluctance in some pockets of British evangelicalism to engage in a defence of Christian truth. This is sometimes manifested in a profound lack of interest in and even a suspicion of the discipline of persuasion.

In a critique of apologetics and persuasion, I recently heard this famous Spurgeon quote:

> Defend the Bible – I would as soon defend a Lion. Open the door and let the lion out; he will take care of himself. Why, they are gone! He no sooner goes forth in his strength than his assailants flee. The way to meet infidelity is to spread the Bible. The answer to every objection against the Bible is the Bible.[9]

Spurgeon was probably right to encourage preachers to be confident and undistracted when expounding Scripture, and to avoid devoting too much pulpit time to the higher criticism that was sweeping all before it. However, the Victorian church was in real and urgent need of apologists who would defend the Bible from this particular enemy. And in the present day, just as lethal weapons and hostile attitudes have put actual lions on the endangered species list, so too biblical Christianity in the West has been systematically removed from vast tracts of the public space and attacked on so many fronts that it is rarely sighted outside the protected confines of church meetings.

Christian parents with children at secondary school are acutely aware that orthodox Christian faith is variously ignored and attacked in both science and humanities lessons, leaving Christian pupils feeling like 'flat-earthers'. There is also an all-pervasive, secular (typically left-wing liberal) atmosphere in Western schools which deems Christian sexual ethics to be regressive and dangerous. How do Christian teenagers survive in this corrosive and toxic atmosphere, in which they are implicated in crimes of homophobia, transphobia and general intolerance simply for believing the Bible?

Often they survive by living alternately in two watertight compartments. They have a Christian compartment for home and church, but at school and with their friends they inhabit the same

secular space as everyone else: one in which science removes the
need for God and approval of gay marriage is the shibboleth they
must utter to be accepted as citizens of a new, more civilized and
tolerant society. Can our Christian youth truly flourish as authentic
and whole people when they are forced to tear themselves in two
merely to survive? Is it any wonder that so many Christian young
people fall away during their teenage years? It is patently obvious to
them that Christian leaders need either to step up and defend the
Bible to a watching world and commend Christianity as true, relevant
and beautiful, or (if they cannot do this) stop demanding that young
people should embrace an outmoded dogma that is increasingly
toxic to their friends.

History Repeats Itself

George Eliot was, like Spurgeon, a product of nineteenth-century
evangelical piety, but unlike him she was undone by the sort of
higher criticism which he had dismissed in the speech quoted above.
She was typical of a whole generation who grew up when evangelicalism was at its most influential. In 1861, on census Sunday,
50% of the English population was in church and evangelicals
had a position of growing prominence. Evangelicals led the way in
philanthropy and social reform; evangelical missionaries had reached
the far-flung reaches of empire such as New Zealand and Australia.
The founding of the Cambridge Inter-Collegiate Christian Union
(CICCU) in 1877 and C.T. Studd's invitation in 1882 to Moody and
Sankey to take the CICCU Mission were markers of this evangelical
momentum and of confidence in the simple 'uncaged' gospel that
evangelicals lived and preached.

Yet at this time of great influence and impact, evangelicalism was
under threat. Like a ship holed below the waterline, evangelicalism
had suffered a mortal blow. Within a generation, the children of
evangelicals had become secularized. They no longer believed what
their parents did.

Even though they had been brought up on the simple gospel
(the wonderful gospel of Christ crucified) both at home and in
church, many had intellectually embraced Darwinism, secular philosophy and higher theological criticism. The Christian home and

the evangelical church were in competition with an emerging secular society, a competition for the hearts and minds of the next generation.

An entire generation was slipping away because many could no longer believe the Bible's teaching was true and relevant in the face of such attacks. The church was largely uninterested in engaging properly with these issues, leaving the lion at the mercy of ruthless hunters.

Monkeys and Bishops

In 1860 at a low-profile (though now famous) public meeting at the Oxford Pitt Rivers Museum, the liberal Bishop of Oxford, Samuel Wilberforce, both insulted the proponents of Darwinism and displayed ignorance by asking Thomas Huxley if his monkey ancestry was on his grandfather's or grandmother's side. This supercilious attack not only showed the churches' ignorance of Darwin's work but also revealed an underlying complacency and arrogance in the face of alternative views.

Leslie Stephen (whose father, Sir James Stephen, had been a prominent member of the evangelical Clapham Sect) had struggled with modern society's objections to original sin and subsequently abandoned all faith.[10] His daughter, Virginia Woolf, continued this reaction against evangelical ethics and belief. She deliberately parodied her grandfather's Clapham Sect by helping to form the Bloomsbury Group, which in turn laid the intellectual and cultural foundations for a post-Christian sexuality. Virginia Woolf in her writing experimented with the idea of both gender and sex being fluid. Her novel *Orlando*,[11] while based on her lover and fellow member of Bloomsbury, Vita Sackville-West, is thought to be exploring gender and transsexual themes and is often referred to in modern transgender studies. Astonishingly, this leading evangelical family moved intellectually, from Clapham to Bloomsbury in barely two generations. And tragically, the Stephens were only one of many to make this journey.

At this critical time the lion was vulnerable and needed to be robustly defended against ruthless hunters who were committed to declawing it and bringing it to the brink of extinction. Tragically, the evangelical church did not seem to have the categories or contact

points to engage with and refute some of the false ideas that were
sweeping away a generation of young Christian believers.

Nothing dramatic seemed to happen in either church or society
in the light of this drift. For the most part, British society continued
to hold onto Christian ethics even though the biblical foundations had been dug out from underneath. George Eliot 'rejected
Christianity not to espouse a philosophy of hedonism or self-
indulgence, but for the far harder task of trying to lead a selfless and
moral life without any Divine assistance'.[12] The Bloomsbury Group,
while rejected as deviant by a morally 'Christian' society, regarded
its own progressive sexual ethic as more intellectually consistent
than the baseless moral assertions of a (now nominally) Christian
society.

With the biblical basis for Christian morality so undermined by
secular intellectual forces, it was only a matter of time before this
unsupported edifice of Christian ethics was toppled.

The student radicals of the 1950s and 1960s not only ushered in
the sexual revolution, but subsequently (from positions of power
and influence) shaped both the political and cultural landscape with
instincts that were hostile to the Christian world view. The new
sexual ethic does not merely ignore the Judaeo-Christian heritage
of self-imposed restraint outside heterosexual marriage, but advocates
that desire and consent now constitute a sufficient basis for sexual
behaviour.

Compromise or Withdrawal?

In the West we now find ourselves at a point where the secularists
are within touching distance of destroying what is left of our Judaeo-
Christian convictions and heritage. How will God's people respond,
especially our Christian leaders and teachers? Typically, the church
has tended to compromise or withdraw. The older denominations are beginning to compromise those foundational truths that
have become so odious to our society, such as the Bible's teaching
on sexuality, the uniqueness of Christ and the realities of heaven
and hell.

Compromise is clearly not an option for true evangelicals whose
view of Scripture is too high to cede both God's creation mandate

and the plain teaching of Jesus for 'the mess of pottage' that is acceptance by a secular society. For those evangelicals who refuse to succumb to the short-sighted appeal of 'open evangelicalism', it seems that we are more likely to withdraw into a personal piety in which we denounce the secular vision as ungodly and circle the wagons in an effort to protect our children.

Indeed, some evangelical leaders seem to suggest that intentional persuasion betrays a lack of dependence on the power and convicting work of the Holy Spirit. At the same time, others are concerned that a persuasion that contextualizes and draws on reason and evidence (not to mention imagination and human longing) is at odds with a proper confidence in the power of the Bible. These are serious charges and will naturally discourage the wider church from drawing on those resources that will help us to engage with and persuade a hostile, post-Christian society.

History and Scripture suggest that such a withdrawal both diminishes the church's capacity to impact our lost society and is unsuccessful at preventing the next generation of Christians from leaving the Christian bubble and inhabiting the new and seemingly progressive secular landscape. Philip Pullman in writing his famous 'His Dark Materials' trilogy[13] was consciously offering an alternative landscape to the Christian one offered by C.S. Lewis's Narnia chronicles, which Pullman routinely described as 'pernicious, racist and misogynist'.[14] 'His Dark Materials', which have sold nearly twenty million copies worldwide and which will be serialized in 2017 in a multimillion-pound BBC production, deliberately encourage young people to reject Christianity and its attendant sexual ethics. In Pullman's world, the universe is ruled by a senile, viciously sadistic deity whose authority must be replaced by human curiosity and ingenuity. Using the church as an instrument of repression, the 'God' figure has kept us from properly exploring our world and sexuality, and so the Kingdom of God must be overthrown and replaced with 'a republic of heaven'.

The challenge to the church is a stark one: we must form a Christian mind in our young people so they become confident that orthodox Christian faith is true, relevant and good. If we do not persuade the next generation of the truth, relevance and goodness of the kingdom of God, the secularists can be confident that they will capture that generation's hearts and minds and welcome our children to their secular republic.

We need the serious-mindedness, careful research and persuasive communication that Don Carson has modelled in key books in which he has responded to both modern and postmodern attacks on orthodox Christianity. Thousands of us have benefited from the persuasive articulation of orthodoxy in *Scripture and Truth*,[15] *The Gagging of God, Becoming Conversant with the Emerging Church*,[16] *Christ and Culture Revisited*[17] and *The Intolerance of Tolerance*.[18] These are examples of how to give a contextualized and persuasive word back that models serious-minded engagement.

However, we cannot sleep easily in our beds simply because clever people such as Don are marshalling persuasive answers to some of the secular attacks on orthodoxy. We need to take a view on the arguments and approaches he puts at our disposal, take up these tools to defend the sacred deposit that is entrusted to us and be engaged in the battle for hearts and minds. This is a daunting task, and we will not realistically commit to it unless we are convinced that such an approach is biblical.

Communicating to the Hard-Hearted

In Scripture we notice that when God and his messengers have something important to say, they tend to do so engagingly, relevantly and persuasively. In his book *Fool's Talk*,[19] Os Guinness describes how the Lord seems to use questions and other rhetorical devices when hearts are particularly hard: 'Where are you [Adam]?' (Gen. 3:9); 'Who told you that you were naked?' (Gen. 3:11); 'Why are you angry [Cain]? Why is your face downcast? If you do what is right, will you not be accepted?' (Gen. 4:6–7); 'Where is your brother Abel?' (Gen. 4:9); 'What have you done?' (Gen. 4:10).[20]

Guinness also describes how some of the prophets use dramatic devices to engage and persuade. One such is used by the prophet Nathan, who is sent by God to King David to confront him for his adultery with Bathsheba and the subsequent murder of her husband. Nathan, knowing that David's defences would be up, delivered God's message to him by means of a gripping and emotive story. He told David about a rich man taking and killing the pet lamb of his poor neighbour and serving it up to his friends for dinner. Supposing the story was true, David became emotionally drawn into it and interjected, '[T]he man who did this must die!' (2 Sam. 12:5) David had become engaged and adamant about the need to punish a rich and powerful man who abused his position. When Nathan responded to David's outrage with the words 'You are the man!' (v. 7), the impact on David was immediate and life-changing.

Was God's prophet, Nathan, using deception and distorting the word of God? On the contrary, the message conveyed was orthodox and the impact was deep and lasting, as David's response in Psalm 51 reveals. Crucially, Nathan realized that being faithful in delivering God's message was not simply about saying the right words: merely asserting that adultery and murder were sinful and offensive to God. Nathan knew it was incumbent upon him to communicate God's message engagingly and persuasively in order to win David's heart and mind. Having read his context well, he realized he needed a less orthodox approach to fulfil his task.

Jesus and the Pharisees

God's commitment to communicate engagingly and persuasively with his fallen creatures is particularly evident in some of Jesus' encounters with the Pharisees. For instance, in Mark 3:20–29 the Pharisees accuse Jesus of casting out demons in the name and power of Satan. Jesus manages to cut to the heart of their sinful attitude, engaging with them by using a combination of imagination and logic. How can you rob a strong man's house without first tying up the strong man? How can I both be overwhelming Satan and plundering his property *and* doing all this on his behalf? Jesus engages his audience, draws them into the inescapable logic of his argument and then delivers his damning verdict that there can be no forgiveness if people reject what is self-evidently true.

Paul with Jews and Pagans

In the book of Acts we see that Paul shows this same determination to be engaging and persuasive as he seeks to challenge unbelief and commend the Way. Luke describes Paul's style of ministry in twelve different cities in vigorous terms.[21]

Paul persuades, defends, reasons, debates and proves and does so using the categories and artefacts that will most readily connect. In Thessalonica, 'As was his custom, Paul went into the synagogue, and on three Sabbath days he reasoned with them from the Scriptures, explaining and proving that the Messiah had to suffer and rise from the dead' (Acts 17:2–3). It is striking that Luke describes the converts here as those who 'were persuaded' (Acts 17:4).

Paul then moves down the coast a couple of hundred miles and engages with Athenian intellectuals and persuades some that Jesus is both Lord and Judge. With this group Paul famously uses their pagan shrines and poems rather than the Jewish Scriptures. He is confident that he can preach the authentic gospel to Athenians, even without the Scriptures, because truth translates. God as creator, sustainer and judge are revealed truths that can be communicated using pagan imagery. In the only other recorded sermon to pagans (Acts 14:15–17), Paul preaches a similar message to the inhabitants of Lystra, in which he does not appeal to the authority of the text of Scripture. This is not to suggest we use the Bible only when we have to; far from it. Rather, it is to suggest that being faithful to the Bible is fundamentally about communicating its revealed truths engagingly and persuasively.

It is worth noting that Luke does not break stride as he concludes his account of Paul's Areopagus address and moves seamlessly onto Paul's visit to Corinth: 'After this, Paul left Athens and went to Corinth . . . Every Sabbath he reasoned in the synagogue, trying to persuade Jews and Greeks' (Acts 18:1, 4).[22]

Subsequently, when Paul is under arrest and Festus tries to distract him from his engaging and persuasive apologetic, Festus resorts to demeaning abuse (Acts 26:24–25): 'At this point Festus interrupted Paul's defence. "You are out of your mind, Paul!" he shouted. "Your great learning is driving you insane." "I am not insane, most excellent Festus," Paul replied. "What I am saying is true and reasonable."' King Agrippa realizes that Paul is seeking to persuade him to become a Christian and knows that he cannot simply dismiss something so compelling and reasonable. So he replies, 'Do you think that in such a short time you can persuade me to be a Christian?' (Acts 26:28). (NB: If you have not yet read Stefan Gustavsson's and Kirsten Birkett's essays – chapters 4 and 5 respectively – you will find there a fuller treatment of Paul's approach.)

It seems clear that in order to communicate engagingly and persuasively, contextualization is essential. Throughout history the Lord has sent messengers who strove to win hearts and minds. Our own contextualizing additionally takes its cue from God's own radical identification in sending Jesus as a human being.

Faithful to the *Form* of Scripture

Yet at this acute time, when the church is in danger of talking past vast tracts of society, there is still reluctance in some evangelical quarters to contextualize and persuade properly. In our embattled position, we evangelicals can champion 'being faithful' above being effective and thereby excuse ourselves when we fail to engage and communicate, provided that we 'preach the gospel'. What is considered 'faithful' is invariably limited to the *content* of a given passage; were we to be faithful to the *form* in which the prophets and apostles communicated, being persuasive would become a high priority.

Parents would never accept such low standards from a schoolteacher who failed to connect with his entire English exam class when teaching *Hamlet*. Would the teacher dare to excuse his failure to engage students with such a gripping play by pointing out that he could do no more than be faithful to the text?

The logic seems to be that by 'failing to engage and communicate' (so long as we say the right words), we leave the most room for God to show his power by converting people anyway. If we adopt this approach consistently, we will find that our churches and CUs will attract fewer and fewer of the unchurched 90%. Instead, we will be speaking to a well-disposed but tiny fringe whose sympathy to our message confirms that we do not need to work hard at contextualization.

Clyde Kilby is at a loss to know how those of us who love and pore over the Scriptures could be so blind to their imaginative form and content:

Now when we look from these three facts (that the Bible belongs to literature, that the Bible is an imaginative book, that God is the greatest artist of all) to contemporary evangelical Christianity, we find a great oddity.

The people who spend the most time with the Bible are in large numbers the foes of art and the sworn foes of imagination . . . How can it be that with a God who created birds and the blue of the sky who before the foundation of the world wrought out a salvation more romantic than Cinderella, with a Christ who encompasses the highest heaven and deepest hell, with the very hairs of our head numbered, with God closer than hands and feet, Christians often turn out to have an unenviable corner on the unimaginative and the commonplace?

Evangelical Christians have had one of the purest of motives and one of the worst outcomes. The motive is never to mislead by the smallest fraction of an iota in the precise nature of salvation, to live it and state it in its utter purity. But the unhappy outcome has too often been to elevate the cliché. The motive is that the gospel shall not be misunderstood, not sullied, not changed in jot or tittle. The outcome has often been merely reactionary, static, and hackneyed . . . There is a simplicity, which diminishes and a simplicity that enlarges, and evangelicals have often chosen the wrong one.[23]

Modern Echo Chambers and the Loss of Empathy

Recently, there have been some exchanges within conservative evangelical circles about whether there is a place for considered contextualization or whether simply 'teaching the Bible' is sufficient. These have led to some fairly binary responses on social media, in which – it has felt to me – that both sides are primarily speaking into their own echo chambers rather than seeking to win hearts and minds. Echo-chamber communication is part of a wider cultural phenomenon that has not left evangelicals unscathed.

A number of commentators have highlighted just how tribal and bitter the atmosphere in the US Congress has become since Newt Gingrich shortened the congressional working week to three days. The consequence was that many senators and representatives began to commute weekly rather than move to Capitol Hill with their families, where they had previously mixed at school gates and in the neighbourhood. It soon became much easier to demonise political opponents because they were strangers.

The division and disgust in public discourse following both Brexit and the Trump election seem here to stay. Selective news feeds through social media have created a much more binary and Manichaean view of reality. This is a huge challenge for everyone and particularly for the church, which seeks to reach this lost society by identifying, connecting and persuading. We are not going to succeed in this enormous task if we cannot even model an intelligent, generous and yet robust discourse with fellow evangelicals.

Donald Trump on his 2016 presidential campaign trail spoke of 'draining the swamp', and Hilary Clinton referred to Trump supporters as a 'basket-full of deplorables'. Disgust is an indelible ink which is harming both the public discourse and that of evangelical leaders.

Jonathan Haidt in his seminal book *The Righteous Mind*[24] appeals for a new type of empathy to enable those with different political and religious instincts to be able to hear each other and make the public space more civil. Haidt argues convincingly that conservatives and liberals are 'hard-wired' differently and so will instinctively and emotionally incline to a certain position that they will subsequently justify and defend. By contrast, identification and empathy are much more considered, intentional and costly responses. 'You never really understand a person until you consider things from his point of view – until you climb into his skin and walk around in it' (Atticus Finch).[25] 'I have become all things to all people so that by all possible means I might save some. I do all this for the sake of the gospel, that I may share in its blessings . . . Follow my example, as I follow the example of Christ' (1 Cor. 9:22–23; 11:1; the apostle Paul).

The Curiosity of Strangers

In her new book, *Strangers in Their Own Land: Anger and Mourning on the American Right*,[26] Arlie Hochschild (a Berkeley sociology professor of thirty years) seeks to address the failure of many liberals in the USA to pierce what she calls their own political bubble. She did this by spending five years of her life carrying out sociological research in Lake Charles, Louisiana, home to a huge number of Tea Party, and latterly Trump, supporters.

What does Hochschild conclude from her trip into the heartland of the American right?

> It's funny, about empathy, because when I set out on this, people said: 'Oh, going to the South, and talking to Tea Party people. I could never do that. I'd just get too mad.' As for other people, well, I could see the look on their face, as if I was maybe giving in to the other side. Was I a covert right-winger? But this is a misunderstanding of empathy – the idea that it alters the basic you, so you better watch out and not empathize too much; that it's a dangerous thing, giving in to the enemy; or that it's too taxing, too exhausting hiding your feelings. On the contrary, I found my experience enlarging and not in the least exhausting.[27]

Hochschild (a feminist and environmentalist) met a Pentecostal minister's wife (white and middle-aged) who said provocatively, 'Oh, I love Rush Limbaugh' (an influential radio host with extremely right-wing views). Rather than react, Hochschild sat with this woman over tea the next day and asked what it was she liked about Limbaugh: 'Oh, I love it that he hates the feminazis and environmental wackos.' Reflecting on what was a deliberately personal jibe, Hochschild recalls:

> And so I was acting neutral, and taking notes, and then she stopped and said to me: 'Was it hard for you to hear what I had to say?' And I thought, wow, she's watching me. And I said, very honestly: 'No, not at all. I have my alarm system off and the reason I'm here is to learn from you and you're doing me an enormous favour and I can't tell you how much I appreciate it.' And she replied: 'You know, I can turn my alarm system off, too. I know what you're doing – I can do that too.' And then the conversation changed, it became an entirely different conversation. She said: 'You know what I really like about Limbaugh? It's that he protects me from the liberal epithets that you college-educated people on the coast often express toward us working-class Southerners . . . [who] think that I am sexist, racist, homophobic, too religious, uneducated and fat.' And she told me that Rush Limbaugh protected her from all those

epithets. But most interestingly, she could relate to what I was doing. She understood my desire to listen and empathize.[28]

The Deep Story

Hochschild continues:

> Empathy seems to me to be a tool for really entering a worldview, and a perspective, at the bottom of which, are human feelings.
> I came up with the idea of what I call a 'deep story' – we all have it, left, right and centre. What is a deep story? A story of how life feels, what feels true ... It's what TS Eliot called an 'objective relative,' with a core set of feelings.[29]

In Luke 15 Jesus entered the deep story of his most bitter opponents, those who eventually conspired in his arrest and crucifixion. The Pharisees murmured their disgust at Jesus' spending time with tax collectors and sinners rather than with respectable and sound people like themselves. In response, Jesus, recognizing their sense of disgust at and isolation from Jesus' friendship with 'the enemy', told the Pharisees their own deep story.

In the story of the prodigal son it is immediately clear who the bad son is and who the good son is. The prodigal leaves the family, leaves his father, breaks up the family estate and effectively says, 'Dad, I'd be happier if you were dead. I don't want to be with you or work for you. I just want my share of your money.' To a Jewish mind, to take money out of the family business, spend it (probably) on prostitutes and drink and then to end up eating pig food is utterly deplorable. It is to take one beyond the reach of sympathy or rescue.

So when, in the story, the prodigal comes home to scrounge food and a job from his dad, you can imagine the Pharisees emitting a low boo and hiss at his brazen selfishness, for not even having the integrity to live with the consequences of his folly. The great shock is the father running to welcome him and seeming to reward the prodigal for his selfish rebellion with an extravagant celebration.

Jesus has really entered their deep story as he voices the Pharisees' deep outrage through the older brother, who seems to be the only sane character. Jesus effectively says, 'I know how you feel about my welcoming tax collectors and sinners: those who have sold out on being God's chosen people and are either collaborating with the enemy or living like pagans. Your deep story causes you to think I am morally undiscerning and weak by eating and celebrating with them.'

This was the warmest invitation Jesus ever gave the Pharisees in the Gospels and must surely have helped those Pharisees who came to faith later on. Jesus does not merely identify with their deep story. He tells them a deeper story, a bigger and a better story that he invites them to enter. He says, 'Let me pull back the curtain onto the ultimate reality of God's throne. The angels in God's presence are celebrating sinners and tax collectors coming home and the Father invites you to come inside and join in the celebration.' We have to celebrate what God is celebrating, or we remain outside.

Whose Deep Stories Do We Need to Learn?

We must surely learn the deep stories of those in our secular society who have seen Christianity used as an instrument to repress the rights of minorities and to impose religious morality on others. Their anger continues to fuel many of the comments made in mainstream media that so dishearten the younger generation of Christians, who struggle to remain part of something perceived to be so harmful.

We also need specifically to learn the deep stories of the so-called Snowflake generation. My natural instinct is to tell them not to be so soft and to toughen up a bit, which might make me feel better, but will do little to commend the truth, relevance and goodness of the gospel. We need to come close enough to commend them for their concern not to cause harm and distress, and in so doing tell them a deeper story in which true human flourishing will come only by allowing the challenge and discomfort of this dangerous message to open up the way to eternal life and true humanness.

Men despise religion. They hate it and are afraid it may be true. The cure for this is to show that religion is not contrary to reason, but worthy of reverence and respect. Next make it attractive, make good men wish it

were true, and then show that it is. Worthy of reverence because it really
understands human nature. Attractive because it promises true good.[30]

Practically, this means that those of us speaking evangelistically
(beyond the echo chambers of our tiny fringes) must, more than
ever, identify with the position of our imagined protagonist and
show a deeper understanding and empathy before ultimately challenging and confronting what is false. In the 114 UCCF CU mission
weeks last year, of the 46,000 students who attended, the vast
majority were totally unchurched.

My view is that a prevailing apathy to Jesus' claims on student's
lives is diminishing and increasingly giving way to intrigue, shock
and sometimes open-mouthed hostility as Jesus of Nazareth walks
off the pages of Scripture. Jesus is sufficiently unknown to Gen Z
to be interesting, attractive and deeply challenging once more. The
main reason such students are willing to hear about Jesus on campus
is because they are invited by fellow students who are close enough
to them to be trusted.

Uniting Evangelicals around Scripture

We must surely strive to maintain a degree of empathy and respect
for those evangelical brothers and sisters with whom we disagree
about this. Current leaders will no doubt be affected by the hostile
spirit of identity politics that is all around us and find it increasingly
hard to mirror the cooperative and generous spirit of those evangelical leaders who grew up during the war years.

If we are to model epistemic humility in our disagreements
with fellow evangelicals, I suggest we must be more curious and
empathetic about what deeper issues might lie under the surface of
this whole debate. On the one hand, there is a genuine and godly
fear among some conservative evangelicals that contextualization
and persuasion may lead to a focus on human wisdom and undermine
the power of Scripture. Are they therefore suggesting that we simply
quote the Bible as if it were a magic incantation to release God's
power? No, I really do not think they are saying that. Those I have
personally spoken to about this have a high view of expository
preaching and would not argue for simply quoting texts of Scripture

in evangelism. On the other side of this debate, those who feel the force of the biblical case for contextualization and persuasion can similarly be caricatured as lacking confidence in the Bible, when in reality it is their high view of the form and content of Scripture that compels them to work hard at conveying its message effectively.

Putting aside these lazy caricatures, where does the difference lie and can it be resolved biblically?

Christ and Culture Revisited?

In *Christ and Culture Revisited*, Carson makes the point that there are several biblical perspectives on Christ and culture and the notion that sections of the church can choose just one of these is mistaken. If we limit ourselves to a single theme of Scripture by, for example valuing God only as creator but not as redeemer, we are going to diminish and distort God's revelation of himself and not see culture in the context of salvation history. Additionally, we need to place creation and fall together and not neglect the biblical theme of heaven and hell (for example), if we are to achieve a more fully orbed biblical perspective of culture. Carson demonstrates that any approach which either excludes or mishandles these perspectives is going to be inherently flawed and inconsistent with biblical orthodoxy.

In attempting to identify the point of divergence – hopefully without caricaturing those who are disinclined to contextualize – I think there is a profound neglect of the doctrine of creation and especially the biblical doctrine of humanity at the heart of all this. The great fear that contextualization and persuasion may diminish our confidence in the Bible and even distort its message seems to come from an unnecessarily sharp disjunction between God's words and human words. God's written Word itself is of course a historically contingent document that requires human enterprise to be established, translated, interpreted and applied. This is in sharp contrast to the Islamic view of the Qur'an, which denies any contribution from human intelligence and interpretation.

The God of the Bible does not speak to us in ways that are unmediated by either the created order or human activity. If God wanted to do this he could, but he chooses not to (e.g. Matt. 19:4), because the created order and human activity have been designed to communicate the words of God. For critics of persuasion and contextualization to say (effectively) 'You contextualize and persuade and I will just preach' is to labour under a false dichotomy that minimizes the human aspects of biblical communication. At best this position is naive, but at worst it involves denying a key aspect of our humanity, since it is suggesting that there is a way for our words to transcend our finite nature and to become divine in some unalloyed way. To say 'I don't contextualize' is to say, 'I'm not subject to the same kind of cultural limitations that constrain normal human beings.' To say 'I just preach the Bible' is to say, 'My reading is not subject to the kind of limitations that other human beings experience.'[31] This is dangerous territory indeed, since it places us on the creator side of the creator–creature distinction. To be more spiritual than the Bible is ultimately to diminish our humanness, which will eventually make our faith look odd and sectarian.

This underlying neglect and even suspicion of the created order seems to champion a division between God and creation rather than between God and sin. If it is possible to be a creature and not sin, which the Incarnation shows it is, then we need not be afraid of creaturely means of contextualization and persuasion, but only of their sinful misuse. In order correctly to discern the relationship between Christ and culture, Carson says that we must 'pursue with a passion the robust and nourishing wholeness of biblical theology as the controlling matrix for our reflection on the relations between Christ and culture'.[32]

As we seek to commend the gospel as true, relevant and good and the only basis for true human flourishing, we must surely work harder at understanding our secular society and be able to live and speak a better and deeper story. We must both demonstrate that our churches and CUs are loving and kind communities, and declare that all of us are guests of a bigger reality as we hear God's claim upon our hearts, minds and bodies. That is, we have a dangerous message to deliver within a safe space. Once again the church must not only outlive but also out-think her pagan contemporaries.

Notes

1. D.A. Carson, *The Gagging of God: Christianity Confronts Pluralism* (Grand Rapids, Mich.: Zondervan, 1996).

2. D.A. Carson, *How Long, O Lord? Reflections on Suffering and Evil* (Leicester: Inter-Varsity Press, 1990).

3. There was a social media storm in September 2016 when the London School of Economics Christian Union put on a Fresher's Barbecue for the men and Tea for the ladies.

4. Tracy McVeigh, 'Peter Tatchell: Snubbed by Students for Free Speech Stance', *The Guardian*, 13 February 2016. Ben Quinn, 'Petition Urges Cardiff University to Cancel Germaine Greer Lecture', *The Guardian*, 23 October 2015.

5. 'Free Speech University Rankings', *Spiked Online* <http://www.spiked-online.com/free-speech-university-rankings/analysis#.WCyAS2crGZV>.

6. Michael J. Boskin, 'Four Lessons from Donald Trump's US Election Victory', *The Guardian*, 13 December 2016.

7. According to Google, 'Generation Snowflake or Snowflake Generation is a term that refers to young people, typically university or college students, who seek to avoid emotionally charged topics or dissenting ideas and opinions. This may involve support of safe spaces and trigger warnings in the university setting' <http://www.rynoreport.com/single-post/2016/11/16/Melting-Snowflakes>.

8. Benjamin Franklin, 'Reply to the Governor', Pennsylvania Assembly, 11 November 1755.

9. From a speech at the Annual Meeting of the British and Foreign Bible Society, 5 May 1875.

10. Ian C. Bradley, *The Call to Seriousness: The Evangelical Impact on the Victorians* (London: Macmillan, 1976), p. 200.

11. Virginia Woolf, *Orlando* (London: Hogarth, 1928).

12. Bradley, *Call*, p. 199.

13. Philip Pullman, *Northern Lights, The Subtle Knife* and *The Amber Spyglass*, 3rd ed. (New York: Scholastic, 2011).

14. John Ezard, *Guardian Online*, 3 June 2002.

15. D.A. Carson and John D. Woodbridge (eds.), *Scripture and Truth* (Grand Rapids, Mich.: Zondervan, 1983).

16. D.A. Carson, *Becoming Conversant with the Emerging Church: Understanding a Movement and Its Implications* (Grand Rapids, Mich.: Zondervan, 2005).

17. D.A. Carson, *Christ and Culture Revisited* (Grand Rapids, Mich.: Eerdmans; Nottingham: Apollos, 2008).

18. D.A. Carson, *The Intolerance of Tolerance* (Grand Rapids, Mich.: Eerdmans, 2012).

19. Os Guinness, *Fool's Talk: Recovering the Art of Christian Persuasion* (Downers Grove, Ill.: InterVarsity Press, 2015).

20. Bible quotations in this chapter are from the New International Version (2011 ed.).

21. Damascus, 9:22; Jerusalem, 9:28–29; Antioch, 13:26–33; Thessalonica, 17:2–4; Berea, 17:10–12; Athens, 17:17; Corinth, 18:4; Ephesus, 18:19; 19:8–9; Miletus, 20:20–21; Jerusalem, 22:1–21; Caesarea, 26:24–27; Rome, 28:23–24.

22. See Stefan Gustavsson's chapter in this volume, which tackles Paul's denial that he used wise and persuasive words in Corinth.

23. Clyde S. Kilby, 'The Bible as a Work of Imagination', in Leland Ryken (ed.), *The Christian Imagination: The Practice of Faith in Literature and Writing* (Colorado Springs, Colo.: Shaw, 2002), p. 105.

24. Jonathan Haidt, *The Righteous Mind: Why Good People Are Divided by Politics and Religion* (London: Penguin, 2012).

25. Harper Lee, *To Kill a Mockingbird* (New York: Hachette, 1982), p. 30.

26. Arlie Hochschild, *Strangers in Their Own Land: Anger and Mourning on the American Right* (New York: The New Press, 2016).

27. Interview with Arlie Hochschild, 29 November 2016 <http://www.spiked-online.com/newsite/author/Arlie%20Hochschild>.

28. Ibid.

29. Ibid.

30. Pascal, *Pensées* (London: Penguin, 2003).

31. Graham Shearer, unpublished writings, 2016, used with permission.

32. Carson, *Christ and Culture*, p. 227.

9. UNIVERSITY MISSIONS
AND EVANGELISM TODAY

Tim Keller and Michael Keller

Don Carson has, his entire life, been an ardent proponent of and participant in university missions. Both of us are also passionate about this subject and have had some years of experience in student evangelism. Tim became a Christian through the ministry of InterVarsity Christian Fellowship in 1970–1, and later served as InterVarsity associate staff. More recently he was a missioner at the University-wide Oxford Inter-Collegiate Christian Union (OICCU) missions in 2012 and 2015. Michael has been the director of City Campus Ministry in New York City, a chapter of Reformed University Fellowship, for the past seven years, and became a Christian through the same ministry while at Vanderbilt University. He accompanied his father on both OICCU mission weeks.

Evangelism on campus is not for the faint of heart. It has always been controversial. Speaking at one of the earliest university-wide evangelistic events sponsored by the OICCU, Dr Martyn Lloyd-Jones was mocked by a leading member of the Oxford Union debating society, who thought the sermon an insult to the intelligent. He argued that Lloyd-Jones's preaching was better suited to 'a congregation of farm labourers' than to university students.[1] That was in 1941, and certainly the university environment is far more resistant to student evangelism today. It does not matter. We believe nothing could be more important. Here are our thoughts on why it is imperative and how we can move forward with evangelism on university campuses today.

Its Importance

Why is evangelism among university students so crucial? One reason is because of the unique openness the university experience creates in students' lives. During undergraduate years, young adults usually experience a new level of independence from family and other childhood connections. For many, it is the first time out of the house and being fully responsible for their daily decisions and actions. Most students go to college not to stay the same but to set their own course in life, so there is an openness to big questions and different ideas, even radically new ones. Young adults at this stage of life have always been asking at least four such big questions: Who am I (looking inward)? What's the point or meaning of things (looking outward)? Whom should I be with and love (looking sideways)? And, in the light of the first three answers, what should I do with my life (looking forward)? Those who don't go to college often accept the answers to these issues that their families and home communities assign to them. University students certainly have social pressure on them from their background, but they are given much more space and opportunity to make significant changes.

While students have always wrestled with some form of these basic questions, our late modern secular culture has intensified the dynamics. Consider Amherst College in Massachusetts, which explains its mission like this: 'Since 1821, we've been helping our students find their own voices, discover their own truths and forge their own paths in the world.'[2] It would be hard to find a more blatant expression of what has been called 'expressive individualism'. (And we strongly doubt that the college founders in 1821 thought they were helping students 'discover their own truths'!) Nevertheless, this shows that, more than ever, universities create environments that encourage students to rethink the beliefs of their upbringing, including their meaning in life, values and identity. That of course is a challenge to students who come into undergraduate courses with a Christian faith. It also means, however, that students from other backgrounds and communities are dislodged from them and are freer to consider the claims of Christianity then they would have been at home.

Also, while it may be considered impolite in much of society to try to convert people to your belief system, on university campuses this is essentially what everyone is trying to do to everyone else, with vigour. The free market of ideas and the discussions that ensue inside and outside the lecture room are not value-neutral exchanges, but rather places of persuasion where individuals debate and accept differing explanations of the good, the true and the beautiful. Evangelism fits right in.

Another reason evangelism is crucial during university years should not be overlooked. It concerns time. College students' life patterns give them the kind of time for discussion, questioning, study and enquiry, a luxury that most people do not have. Today's students will insist that they are overwhelmingly busy, but every man or woman who graduates from college and enters the marketplace looks back and realizes that their schedule was actually more flexible than it would ever be again. So we must strike while the iron is hot. University undergraduates have both the freedom and the bandwidth required to consider abandoning one comprehensive set of beliefs about life and adopting a whole new one. Later in their lives their world view 'settles in' through vocational choices and longer-term friendships and new family ties. This makes it far harder to get anything like the focused attention and energy necessary to examine the foundations of one's entire life.

The university, then, is in many ways uniquely suited for evangelism. There is no other place in our culture that affords listeners the space and freedom, time and posture, to talk about the Meaning of It All.

There is one last reason why we should make university evangelism a high priority. Today there are enormous numbers of international students flocking to receive Western educations. One reason we should reach out to them has already been noted. Away from their home cultures and communities they are far more accessible and open to consideration of the claims of Christianity than they ever have been before or, possibly, will be again. Indeed, many students who opt for a Western education have every intention of weighing world-view options and other religions. And there is another thing to bear in mind. A significant percentage of international students return to their countries and assume positions of influence. Colleges always talk about 'training future leaders' but in this case it is largely true. Student evangelists can engage in international missions to dozens of countries without the need for a single passport. There is no better way to 'make disciples of all nations' than to reach international students in our universities.

Its Challenge

While all of these historic advantages for evangelism of students remain, nevertheless, all is not well. A biography of John Stott shows that the large numbers of conversions that British university missioners saw in the 1940s and 1950s diminished markedly in the 1960s and thereafter.[3] After the Second World War the secularism that largely had been confined to European intellectual elites for two hundred years finally broke out into the population at large, especially among the college educated. Its components included the sexual revolution, as well as various liberation movements that stressed the autonomy of the individual. The Marxist critique of social power captured the imaginations of many students. Religion in general and Christianity in particular were implicated by their involvement in historic, unjust social structures. Religion was seen to be an obstruction to human progress and scientific discovery. In more recent decades, especially in Europe and Britain, religion has appeared more and more to be simply irrelevant to leading a good life and making a better world. Nonetheless, Christian student movements continued to grow and even flourish in various parts of the Western world up to the end of the twentieth century.

Some believe, however, that the university may be entering a new era of opposition to student ministry, and particularly to evangelism. When weighing what seems to be the beginning of a shift or trend, it is always hard to know whether it will be localized and temporary or sweeping and lasting. However, particularly in elite American universities, students are becoming highly sensitive: traumatized and outraged by opposing viewpoints.

There has begun a strong movement to control speech on campus and to punish any statements perceived to be bigoted or discriminatory. A discriminatory statement is now defined as that which offends the listener and which is perceived to violate his or her dignity and identity. So, in contrast to former times, students demand no longer only respectful, civil disagreement but full recognition and affirmation. Any failure to provide an environment that keeps dignity 'safe' must be punished, both by college administrators and social media. Don Carson did some reconnaissance on this trend in his 2013 book *The Intolerance of Tolerance*,[4] but it has accentuated almost exponentially even in the last three years into what is now called 'vindictive protectiveness'.

This new climate finds the absolute claims of Christianity, no matter how carefully and warmly expressed, to be a violation of the dignity and identities of others. In a *New York Times* article titled 'In College and Hiding From Scary Ideas', Judith Shulevitz addresses the belief that colleges should keep students safe from distressing viewpoints and therefore from psychological angst. She argues that 'while keeping college-level discussions "safe" may feel good to the hypersensitive, it's bad for them and for everyone else'.[5] Shielded from unfamiliar ideas, students will never learn the discipline of seeing the world through the eyes of someone with a sharply different viewpoint. They will be unable to process new arguments and ideas because their intellectual climate has been so tightly controlled.

The reasons for this change are complex. One is the flowering of an approach to personal identity that no longer looks outward to norms, commitments and communities, but that is wholly inward and individualistic. Charles Taylor, in *The Malaise of Modernity*, explains that this kind of identity is fragile, needs constant affirmation, and, ironically, requires *more* recognition and support from popular opinion.[6] In the past, all conceptions of identity involved connecting to some outside truth bigger than yourself. The contemporary view, however, is that we need no 'truth' other than our own. Religion of any kind is seen as destructive to the unimpeded inward journey necessary to become 'true to one's self'.

In the 1940s, Dr Lloyd-Jones could be nonchalantly dismissed as being simply unenlightened. Today the gospel message is more likely to be taken seriously as a threat to freedom and the full expression of personal identity.

Another root of the new 'weaponized tolerance' is the convoluted moral relativism of our culture, which is an entailment of the individualistic identity. Morality is now seen to have no grounding except in one's personal feelings. There is no moral source outside the self to which two people could have recourse in order to come to some agreement on an ethical issue. Sociologist Christian Smith shows how this makes young American adults essentially schizophrenic. On the one hand, they are often moralistic, with vehement convictions that some practices are very, very wrong. But almost in the same breath they will say that there are no moral absolutes, that everyone must determine what is right or wrong for them.[7] This profound inarticulacy makes it hard for many students to conceive of anything like a 'search for truth' that once marked the university. It also means students can (1) denounce a speaker for his beliefs and views, but (2) then say to their own critics that 'No one has the right to tell anyone what is wrong for them,' and after doing both (3) see absolutely no inconsistency in this at all. To call this a conversation-stopper is putting it mildly. How does a Christian evangelist get traction, not just with moral relativists, but with mora*listic* moral relativists?

Other roots of the current climate lie in trends in popular culture and technology, as detailed by Jonathan Haidt and some others.[8] Perhaps the most obvious and pervasive influence is the Internet. Today's undergraduate students are the first to have spent their entire adolescence on social media, and there has been much analysis about its effects on them.[9] Studies have shown that social media makes relationships controllable but also (and therefore) much 'thinner' and more superficial. Also, by comparison, it makes face-to-face encounters feel much more threatening. For example – how do you just 'block' a critic that is physically standing in front of you? You can't. That is why aggrieved parties have their interchanges online, where they can simply hit the off button to end it. Before hitting the off button, however, Internet communication makes possible the kind of cutting insults and dehumanizing declarations that few people feel able to make to someone's face.

In sum, critics show that the Internet has led to a kind of illiteracy with regard to conflict resolution and committed relationships in general. Even more foreign to the Internet user, for all the reasons just cited, is the very idea of forgiveness. Haidt and others show how, for all these reasons, the Internet has contributed to the tolerant-looking intolerance, the breakdown of dialogue on campus, and the growing outrage and hostility toward religion and toward classical understandings of a virtuous human life.[10]

Its Promise

We hope that the realism of the last section of our chapter does not give the impression that we think the prospects for university missions and evangelism are bleak. Not at all. The current climate, for all of its challenges, also provides promising opportunities.

First, there is a deeper hunger for relationships than ever. Students still intuitively want deeper friendships and relationships than their culture affords or encourages. Students are very lonely and much more anxious than earlier generations.[11] If they experience, not the thinness of late modern consumer networking, but real friendship and love, they will be strongly attracted to it, despite the fact that these relationships are harder for them to manage. Yes, they are afraid of commitment, can easily take offence and can simply disappear without a word or notice if they get overwhelmed or anxious. However, evangelists who are really motivated by love will not be put off or daunted. A patient evangelist, who is not him- or herself fragile and easily hurt, and who offers a tireless, listening ear, will gain a hearing. Student evangelism has always stressed the importance of relationship but, in our time, love will be as important as argument for showing people the plausibility of the gospel. Student workers will have no more important skill than the ability to maintain as many non-perfunctory, caring relationships as possible.

Secondly, there is a genuine concern about the lack of moral sources in secularism. Long ago Nietzsche pointed out how deeply incoherent secular liberalism is. Most forms of modern secularism insist that the universe is purposeless, that there is no supernatural, transcendent dimension, that we are here only through a process of the strong eating the weak, and that there is no afterlife or final judgment for our behaviour. They then turn around and, in the same breath, insist even more loudly that every human being has inviolable dignity and rights, that we must care for the welfare of all people, that we must alleviate poverty, hunger, disease, injustice and suffering everywhere it exists.

These two beliefs – in materialism *and* humanistic moral values – are utterly contradictory, as Nietzsche and scores of other thinkers have pointed out. This could be the secular 'Achilles heel'. Students will not see this immediately, however. They are so fully habituated to see these beliefs as compatible that they will not immediately perceive the problem. Overzealous, triumphalistic evangelists who seem to be saying that atheists cannot be moral people will only arouse students' ire. It is important to give full credit to moral, secular individuals, while also showing the lack of moral sources within the secular world view to support the very ethical and justice commitments they have. Done well, this *is* something that can trouble students in ways that lead to fruitful lines of enquiry. We have seen it many times. It is not comfortable to be moralistic moral relativists, as so many students are. However, as we said above, it is much easier to convince them of the problem in private, personal dialogues than in public debates or impersonal mass communication. These will almost inevitably draw the charge that 'you think only Christians can be good'.

Thirdly, there is the powerful witness of graciousness. As we have observed, communication in contemporary culture is increasingly shrill. Opinions are seldom expressed without being accompanied by denunciations, condemnation and disdain for the contrary position. Ironically, these are the ugly marks of Pharisaism, the self-righteousness of religious pride. It is the result of the profound spiritual anxiety that belongs to those who are trying to prove themselves and save themselves, whether they are formally religious or not. Christian evangelists who exhibit a radically different spirit will stand out. Evangelists, of course, will be testifying to the existence of moral absolutes, but if they do it with obvious graciousness and humility, it will be deeply counter-intuitive for students, yet attractive. This humble-boldness can only come from the knowledge that one is *simul justus et peccator*, both sinful yet infallibly loved. By being courageous and plain-spoken, but gracious and kind at the same time, the evangelist becomes a powerful, disarming, living embodiment of salvation by grace, not works.

Finally, here is the best news of all: Jesus himself is still a compelling figure for students. Exposing students to the person, life and teachings of Jesus, either through direct Bible study and reading, or through the vivid exposition of biblical texts, continues to be the best 'method' of evangelism. In an era that is arguably more open to the imagination than to rational argument, nothing is more effective than to plunge a student into Gospel narratives until Jesus begins to appear in his or her mind's eye. In years past, as with the John Stott university missions of the 1950s, presenting the biblical Christ to students could be almost the whole of evangelism. We believe that today this must be accompanied by more apologetics than was necessary in those times. Nevertheless, showing students Jesus is still the meat of the ministry meal.

Here is one more thought for our encouragement. When Lloyd-Jones was criticized for preaching to undergraduates as if they were simple farm hands, the Doctor responded that Oxford students were 'just ordinary common human clay and miserable sinners like everybody else', and therefore their needs were 'precisely the same as those of the agricultural labourer'.[12] We doubt that this bold retort convinced his critic. But we are grateful that it has been preserved, because all of us who care about university mission and evangelism must never forget it. It does not matter how learned, sophisticated, jaded, postmodern and sceptical contemporary students are. At bottom, their spiritual needs are the same as everyone else's. Their sin and pride are not more impervious to the gospel than those of other classes and other generations. Their hearts must be and can be opened up by God to the truth just like anyone else's (Acts 16:14).

Its Methods

In this environment, with its distinct challenges and opportunities, how should we go about our task? Is there anything practical we can say? Here are a few thoughts.

1. More than ever, students will be won to faith through personal, long-term friendships and dialogues.

We are afraid that readers will think this statement to be too obvious and will not stop to consider its practical implications. In one sense this has always been true. But we have made the case here that personal, relationship-embedded evangelism is more important than ever. British universities have so far escaped the multiplication of campus groups that is the norm in the US, which means that the Christian Union (CU) can be just that: a union of Christians from all sorts of churches who form a genuine mission community. For the average secular student, meeting real Christians in halls of residence, teaching groups or sports teams who become long-term friends is a game changer. Accompanying a Christian friend to a lunchtime dialogue put on by the CU, where a hot topic is skilfully and sympathetically addressed and questions can be asked over a simple, shared lunch, has become incredibly popular. It is the quality of the friendship and the warmth of the atmosphere that creates a 'safe space' in which to discuss a dangerous topic.

Students are more likely to ignore mass communication campaigns but will come to events if invited by Christian friends. Over a hundred CU missions were run in British universities last year and the majority of the 34,000 students who attended a mission event (such as a lunch bar) were brought and followed up by their Christian friends. The best way to tease out their real questions, and to get them to trust the messenger and be willing to investigate Christianity, will be to build a meaningful, personal relationship with them.

This is not to say that public evangelistic events with a speaker cannot be fruitful, because clearly they have been, especially in the UK context of creative, student-run CU events weeks. But more and more, they will be fruitful only if the non-Christians present are not first- or second-time guests, but students who have been in process, in one-on-one evangelistic friendships.

2. More than ever, Christian evangelists will have to be as much 'students of culture' as traditional missionaries have been.

Again the danger is that this statement will seem too obvious. The reason we say this is that cultural trends and generational shifts are occurring at a pace never before seen. Young adults in their mid-20s confess that they can barely relate to the attitudes and beliefs of incoming freshers, only seven years their junior. Exhibit A is the massive, seemingly overnight shift in public attitudes toward sexuality, which have left so many evangelicals in shock, but that is only the most famous example. Many of the main barriers and objections students have to Christianity will change very quickly going forward. This means that Christian evangelists, even if they are relatively recent graduates of the same university where they minister, must assume the stance of 'missionaries' who must learn a new language and culture to communicate the gospel. Of course, like every missionary who ever lived, the campus evangelist must adapt without compromising the gospel message. That is the challenge for Christian evangelists at universities in the West.

3. The two main ways to show Jesus to the students are still the meat of student ministry.

We have said that, in a culture that puts more emphasis on imagination than rationality, it is more important than ever to take students into the stories about Jesus in the Gospels, until they begin to 'see' Jesus. The two ways to do this are still (1) reading the Bible with them one-on-one or in groups, and (2) expounding the biblical texts vividly to them. We mention 'vividly' because we believe contemporary students especially require Bible expositors to bring the scriptural truths home to hearts, not just to the intellect.[13] While we must always forge fresh versions of these two fundamental approaches, they are always the fundamental means to do evangelism on college campuses. In recent years the emergence of Uncover* (a set of evangelistic Bible studies set in a 'cool' pocket-sized version of Luke or John's Gospel) has meant that many of the students attending events have already been reading a Gospel with a Christian friend and are ready to hear and respond to public proclamation. The widespread uptake of one-to-one or small-group seeker studies has also created a generation of graduates who are confident in using the Bible in evangelism because they have seen Jesus walk off the pages of Scripture into the lives of fellow students.

4. Apologetics are important, but they should go beyond the older evidentialist forms and must be woven naturally into every aspect of student ministry.

We have already said that we think apologetics must play a greater role today. Evangelism proper is the answer to the 'what' question: What is the gospel? Apologetics is the answer to the 'why' question: Why should I believe that? Look at John Stott's classic *Basic*

Christianity,[14] based on his mission talks at British universities in the early 1950s. Those talks are masterful, but they rightly assumed in their audience at least a rudimentary belief in the existence of God, and of sin, and of moral norms. He does a remarkable job of clearly laying out the answer to the 'what' question. But today many if not most student listeners will ask, 'Why should we believe what the Bible says about him?' That leads naturally to apologetics regarding the reliability of the Gospels, and perhaps also to the evidence for the resurrection (to which, to be fair, Stott gives some attention).

But those older kinds of 'evidentialist' apologetics, while fine and helpful, are insufficient. Everything Stott says in those talks militates today not just against a scientific mindset that wants empirical proof, but also against deeply held cultural narratives, such as how identity is formed and the nature of freedom. *Basic Christianity* will just seem nonsensical to a student if you do not make those contemporary narratives visible, challenge them and show how Christianity gives a better account of how human life can be understood and lived. This too can be rightly called apologetics, because it removes barriers to belief and clears the way for students to consider the claims of Jesus. Students need to see how Christianity compares to secularism and other religions in its resources for meaning, satisfaction, freedom, identity, justice and hope, things that no human being can live without. Making such comparisons, and critiquing the dominant cultural narratives surrounding each of these concepts, is the work of an apologist.

Student workers should all be skilled in doing this. They should not only rely on apologetics experts to come in, speak and 'mow down' objections to Christianity. Many of today's students will be helped by those kinds of apologetics presentations, but more or most will simply hit the off button. It is in relationships that this generation will be persuaded.

5. Evangelistic events should be marked by variety, vulnerability and often, also, by a light touch.

Despite all our caveats, we believe it is important to have public evangelistic events on campus. One reason is that students need models of how to do Christian persuasion, and skilful speakers provide them. Also, as we said previously, the traditional university mission with an evangelistic speaker can still be very effective if the relational groundwork has been done. But remember that this relational groundwork is ten times more important for the success of university missions than it was a generation ago.

However, there is more to do than simply the relational and traditional. Here are three other examples of public outreach events.

At Columbia University Tim and a Columbia University professor, a well-respected atheist, Philip Kitcher, were invited to address the question 'Do you have to be a good person to have a good life?'[15] After each of us gave opening remarks, a member of the Columbia faculty (who was not an evangelical) chaired a discussion between us and then fielded questions for us from the audience.

A very different kind of event was one that Michael did every semester with RUF City Campus Ministry. It was called 'Stump the Chump'. Christian students invited sceptical friends to come and try to 'stump' the campus minister (Michael). They were to ask him any question or pose any objection to Christianity and have him try to answer it. Then the entire room would vote on whether they believed he had been stumped or had answered pretty well. (You could vote 'answered well' even if you did not agree with the answer.) Sometimes prizes were given to a student who the room thought had stumped Michael. He put himself on the hot seat like this at least once a semester. It was very disarming both by being light-hearted and by making the Christian speaker somewhat vulnerable. It made dialogue and discussion of spiritual issues much less threatening. Yet it was also a way for Michael to present the claims of Christ clearly to many non-believing students.

A final example was organized around John Patitucci, who at the time was a Professor of Music at City College in New York City. John is a believer and a famous jazz bass player. We held an evening called 'The Spiritual Music of John Coltrane'. John Coltrane is the late, legendary jazz saxophonist who claimed to have a religious experience of the love of God that changed his approach to music. We advertised it by email to the jazz music community of New York City and especially to music students at the college. That night John Patitucci and a jazz group performed a 45-minute concert of Coltrane music. Then Tim interviewed John about his faith and how his experience of God's saving grace had changed his attitude toward his music and toward everything else in his life. Tim was given time to provide brief summaries of the gospel. Finally, we took questions from the audience. We estimate that three or four hundred non-Christian jazz musicians were present that night.

What did these events have in common? One was vulnerability. In each case the gospel communicator was not standing 'six feet above contradiction'. None was a simple monologue. There were ways for people to 'talk back'. A second quality was a note of humour or joy. Even the Columbia forum was fortunately not all sombre and formal because my conversation partner was friendly and relaxed and willing to laugh. Finally, these venues were creative and innovative. Non-Christian students found them intriguing and unlike the more stilted and self-important Christian presentations they might have been exposed to in the past.

There is no greater mission field than the university today. Student evangelism has never been more challenged or more needed.

Notes

1. Andrew Atherstone, 'Oxford's 25 Missions', *Evangelicals Now*, February 2015 <https://www.e-n.org.uk/2015/02/features/oxfords-25-missions>.
2. <https://www.amherst.edu/amherst-story>.
3. See ch. 2, 'Students', in Alister Chapman, *Godly Ambition: John Stott and the Evangelical Movement* (Oxford: Oxford University Press, 2014), pp. 33–50.
4. D.A. Carson, *The Intolerance of Tolerance* (Nottingham: Inter-Varsity Press, 2012; repr. Grand Rapids, Mich.: Eerdmans, 2013).
5. <http://www.nytimes.com/2015/03/22/opinion/sunday/judith-shulevitz-hiding-from-scary-ideas.html>.
6. Charles Taylor, *The Malaise of Modernity* (Concord, Ont.: Anasi, 1991).
7. See especially Christian Smith, *Lost in Transition: The Dark Side of Emerging Adulthood* (Oxford: Oxford University Press, 2011).
8. See Greg Lukianoff and Jonathan Haidt, 'The Coddling of the American Mind', in *The Atlantic*, September 2015; Jonathan Haidt, 'Where Microaggressions Really Come From: A Sociological Account', on *The Righteous Mind* website <http://righteousmind.com/where-microaggressions-really-come-from>; Bradley Campbell and Jason Manning, 'Microaggression and Moral Culture', *Comparative Sociology* 13.6, pp. 692–726.

9. Probably the best and most prominent critic of social media in these respects is Sherry Turkle of MIT. See her *Alone Together: Why We Expect More from Technology and Less from Each Other* (New York: Basic, 2012) and *Reclaiming Conversation: The Power of Talk in a Digital Age* (London: Penguin, 2015). See also Nancy Jo Sales, *American Girls: Social Media and the Secret Lives of Teenagers* (New York: Alfred A. Knopf, 2016).

10. As already indicated, these trends are much more realized on elite American college campuses. Our experience is that European and Australian college students are more secular yet less prone to high sensitivity and outrage. Nevertheless, globalization in general and social media in particular seem likely to spread these outlooks, even if national differences will remain in how they play out in different countries.

11. For statistics on the growing number of student mental health problems, see the Jonathan Haidt articles cited previously.

12. Atherstone, 'Oxford's 25 Missions'.

13. For an important book seeking to move expository preaching more in this direction, see Josh Moody and Robin Weekes, *Burning Hearts: Preaching to the Affections* (Fearn: Christian Focus, 2014).

14. John R.W. Stott, *Basic Christianity*, 2nd ed. (Grand Rapids, Mich.: Eerdmans, 1971).

15. This is not, by the way, the same as the question 'Can you be good without God?' For Dr Kitcher and most of the audience that would have been an offensive question. Rather, the issue was whether one could live life well without some kind of moral norms.

10. DOING MISSIONS WHEN DYING IS GAIN

John Piper

Though I am Don Carson's elder (by eleven months), and count him a personal friend, I revere him both spiritually and academically. The level at which Don works in the academic guild is beyond my ability and bent. I stand outside and below, looking up with profound admiration and respect. Make no mistake, my admiration is not awakened by fame and notoriety. It rises for real excellence and faithfulness and usefulness. Don has taken the bricks and mortar of his academic trade and built structures where God's people have found safety and nourishment and joy and power.

Years of working side by side with Don in various ways have taken this academic reverence that I feel and deepened it into a tender, deep, heartfelt esteem for his spiritual authenticity. Don undergoes no metamorphosis moving from the lectern to the prayer meeting, or from the Greek Testament to the university mission. He is as likely to pray for my children as he is to propose a conference.

His burden for the global church is weighty and informed. His international commitments for preaching are unparalleled by other scholars of his stature. His knowledge of the state of evangelicalism around the world regularly amazes me.

For all these reasons, it is an honour to contribute to this special collection on the occasion of his seventieth birthday.

For the Joy of All Peoples

My mission statement in life – and the mission statement of the church I served for 33 years from 1980 to 2013 – is, 'We exist to spread a passion for the supremacy of God in all things for the joy of all peoples through Jesus Christ.'

I love that mission statement for several reasons. One is because I know it cannot fail. I know it cannot fail because it is a promise from Jesus. 'And this gospel of the kingdom will be proclaimed throughout the whole world as a testimony to all nations, and then the end will come' (Matt. 24:14).[1] 'Nations' in that verse does not refer to political states. It refers to something like what we call 'people groups', ethnolinguistic groupings, and we may be absolutely certain that every one of them will be penetrated by the gospel to the degree that you can say that a witness, an understandable, self-propagating witness, will be among them and gathered with God's global people in the new heavens and new earth.

Let me give you some reasons why we can bank on that.

The Promise Is Sure

The promise is sure for several reasons.

1. *Jesus never lies.* It was Jesus who said in Matthew 24:35, 'Heaven and earth will pass away, but my words will not pass away.' So this mission, called world evangelization, is going to be completed. It is going to be done, and you can either get on board and enjoy the triumph or you can cop-out and waste your life. You have only those two choices, because there is no middle option such as, 'Maybe it won't succeed, and I can be on the best side by not jumping on board.' That will not happen.

2. *The ransom has already been paid for God's people among all the nations.* According to Revelation 5:9–10, 'Worthy are you to take the scroll and to open its seals, for you were slain, and by your blood you ransomed people for God from every tribe and language and people and nation, and you have made them a kingdom and priests to our

God, and they shall reign on the earth.' They are paid for, and God will not go back on his Son's payment.

I love the story of the Moravians. In northern Germany, two of them were getting on a boat, ready to sell themselves into slavery in the West Indies, if necessary, never to come back again. And as the boat drifted out into the harbour they lifted their hands and said, 'May the Lamb receive the reward of his suffering.' What they meant was that Christ had already bought those people. And they were going to find them. They would preach the gospel to everyone they could, and trust God to call the ransomed to himself.

So we know God's global mission cannot abort, because the debt has been paid for each of God's people everywhere in the world. Those lost sheep, as Jesus called them, that are scattered throughout the world will come in as the Father calls them through the preaching of the gospel (John 11:51–52).

3. *The glory of God is at stake.* 'Christ became a servant to the circumcised to show God's truthfulness, in order to confirm the promises given to the patriarchs, and in order that the Gentiles might glorify God for his mercy' (Rom. 15:8–9). The whole purpose of the incarnation was to bring glory to the Father through the manifestation of his mercy to the nations.

The glory of God is at stake in the Great Commission. Back in 1983 at Bethlehem Baptist Church, Tom Steller – my partner in ministry for 33 years at the church – and I were both met by God in amazing ways. Tom, in the middle of the night, could not sleep, so he got up, put on a John Michael Talbot album and lay down on the sofa, and he heard our theology translated into missions. We had been a glory-of-God-oriented leadership, but we had not yet made sense of missions as we ought to have done. John Michael Talbot was singing about the glory of God filling the earth the way the waters cover the sea, and Tom wept for an hour.

At the same time, God was moving on my wife, Noël, and me to ask, 'What can we do to make our church a launching pad for missions?' Everything came together to make an electric moment in the life of our church, and it all flowed from a passion for the glory of God.

4. *God is sovereign.* In the late 1990s, as I was preaching sequentially through Hebrews, we arrived at Hebrews 6. This is a very difficult

text about whether the people described are Christians or not when they fall away. And in verses 1–3 there is this amazing statement (which is just a tiny piece of the massive biblical evidence for why I am a Calvinist) that says, 'Let us leave the elementary doctrine of Christ and go on to maturity . . . And this we will do, *if God permits.*' When we looked at this together, there fell across my congregation the most amazing silence. They heard the implications of the words 'if God permits'. Naturally they asked, 'You mean God might not permit a body of believers to press on to maturity?'

God is sovereign. He is sovereign in the church, and he is sovereign among the nations. One testimony to this is in that memorable article in *Christianity Today* years ago retelling the story of Jim Elliot, Nate Saint, Pete Flemming, Roger Youderian and Ed McCully. Steve Saint, Nate's son, tells the story of his dad getting speared by Waorani Indians in Ecuador. He tells it after having learned new details of intrigue in the Waorani tribe that were responsible for this killing. These new details implied that the killings were very unlikely. They simply should not have happened. They made no sense. Yet they did happen. And having discovered the intrigue, he wrote this article. There was one sentence that absolutely blew me out of my living room chair. He said, 'As [the Waorani] described their recollections, it occurred to me how incredibly unlikely it was that the palm beach killing took place at all. It is an anomaly that I cannot explain outside of divine intervention.'

Do not miss that. He says, 'I can explain the spearing of my dad only by virtue of divine intervention.' Do you hear what this son is saying? 'God killed my dad.' He believes that, and I believe that. According to Revelation 6:10–11, when you have a glimpse of the throne room and the martyrs who shed their blood for the gospel saying, '[H]ow long before you will judge and avenge our blood?' the answer comes back, 'Then they were each given a white robe and told to rest a little longer, until the number of their fellow servants and their brothers should be complete, who were to be killed as they themselves had been.' God says, 'Rest until the number that I have appointed is complete.' He has in mind a certain number of martyrs. When it is complete, then the end will come. God is sovereign over the best and worst that happens in world missions. Therefore, the mission cannot fail.

The Price Is Suffering

The price of God's global mission is suffering, and the volatility in the world today against the church is not decreasing. It is increasing especially among the groups that need the gospel. There is no such thing as a 'closed country'. That notion has no root or warrant in the Bible, and it would have been unintelligible to the apostle Paul, who laid down his life in every city he visited.

I remember one Sunday when our church was focusing on the suffering church, and many across the nation were involved. We saw videos or heard stories about places such as Sudan, where the Muslim regime was systematically ostracizing, positioning and starving Christians so that there were about 500 martyrs a day in Sudan. In the light of this, I got very tired of candidates for staff positions in our inner-city church asking, 'Will our children be safe?' I have grown tired of such American priorities infecting the mission of the church. Whoever said that your children will be safe in the call of God?

YWAM (Youth With A Mission) is a wild-eyed, radical group that I love. I got an email from them some years ago saying:

> One hundred and fifty men armed with machetes surrounded the premises occupied by the YWAM team in India. The mob had been incited by other religious groups in an effort to chase them off. As the mob pressed in someone in a key moment spoke up on the team's behalf and they decided to give them 30 days to leave. The team feels they should not leave and that their ministry work in the city is at stake. Much fruit has been seen in a previously unreached region and there is great potential for more. In the past when violence has broken out between rival religious groups people have lost their lives. Please pray for them to have wisdom.

Now this is exactly the opposite of what I mainly hear in America as people decide where to live, for example. I do not hear people saying, 'I don't want to leave, because this is where I'm called to and this is where there's need.' Oh that we might see a reversal of our self-centred priorities! They seem to be woven into the very fabric of our consumer culture: move towards comfort, towards security, towards ease, towards safety, away from stress, away from trouble and away from danger. It ought to be exactly the opposite. It was Jesus himself who said, 'If anyone would come after me, let him . . . take up his cross' (Mark 8:34; cf. Matt. 16:24; Luke 9:23).

It is the absorption of a consumer, comfort, ease culture in the church. And it creates weak ministries and churches in which safe, nice things are done for each other, and safe excursions are made to help save some others. But 'Oh, we won't *live* there, and we won't *stay* there,' not even in America, not to mention Saudi Arabia.

I was in Amsterdam once talking to another wild-eyed, wonderful mission group, Frontiers, founded by another of my heroes, Greg Livingstone. What a great group: 500 people sitting in front of me who risk their lives every day among Muslim peoples. And to listen to them! What a privilege. During the conference they were getting emails, which they would stand up and read, such as, 'Please pray for X. He was stabbed in the chest three times yesterday, and the worst thing is his children were watching him. He's in the hospital in a critical condition.'

Then they would say, 'This is a missionary in the Muslim world; let's pray for him,' and we would go to prayer. Next day another email came, and this time six Christian brothers in Morocco had been arrested. 'Let's pray for them,' the missionaries said; so we did. And so it was throughout the conference. And at the end of it, the missionaries were ready to go back. Am I going to come back to America and be the same? Will I stand up in front of my church and say, 'Let's have nice, comfortable, easy services. Let's just be comfortable and secure'?

Golgotha is not a suburb of Jerusalem. Let us go with him outside the gate and suffer with him and bear reproach (Heb. 13:13).

Suffering Is also the Means

But in saying that there will be martyrs and there must be suffering I have not yet said the main thing about the price of getting the job done. That is because suffering is not just the price of missions but also the means. Here is what I have in my mind: consider Colossians 1:24. 'Now I rejoice', Paul says, 'in my sufferings.' He was a very strange person. 'I rejoice in my sufferings' is very countercultural, very un-American, indeed, very counter-human. 'I rejoice in my sufferings for your sake, and in my flesh I am filling up what is lacking in Christ's afflictions for the sake of his body [that is, the ingathering of God's elect].'

Now that is on the brink of blasphemy. What does he mean by 'filling up what is lacking' in the afflictions of our great God and Saviour, Jesus Christ? How could his afflictions be lacking? Paul does not mean that in his own sufferings he improves upon the merit and the atoning worth of Jesus' blood. That is not what he means. Well then, what does he mean?

There is a remarkable parallel to Colossians 1:24 in Philippians 2:30. What makes it a parallel is the coming together of the same two words, one for 'fill up' (or 'complete') and the other for 'what is lacking'. Paul says that Epaphroditus 'nearly died for the work of Christ, risking his life *to complete what was lacking* in your service to me'.

The situation is that Epaphroditus was sent from the Philippian church over to Paul in Rome. He risked his life to get there, and Paul extols him for risking his life. He tells the Philippians that they should receive such a one with honour, because he was sick unto death and risked his neck to complete their ministry to him.

I opened my 100-year-old Vincent's commentary on Philippians and read an explanation of that verse which I think is a perfect interpretation of Colossians 1:24. Vincent says:

> The gift to Paul from the Philippians was a gift of the church as a body. It was a sacrificial offering of love. What was lacking was the church's presentation of this offering in person. This was impossible, and Paul represents Epaphroditus as supplying this lack by his affectionate, zealous ministry.

So the picture is of a church that wants to communicate love, in the form of money, to Paul in Rome, and they cannot do it. There are too many of them to go and show their love as a group. And it is too far away. So they say, in essence, 'Epaphroditus, represent us and *complete what is lacking in our love*. There's nothing lacking in our love except the *expression* of our love in person there. Take it and communicate it to Paul.'

Now that's exactly what I think Colossians 1:24 means. Jesus dies and he suffers for people all over the world in every nation. Then he is buried and, according to the Scriptures, raised on the third day. Then he ascends into heaven where he reigns over the world. And he leaves a work to be done.

Paul's self-understanding of his mission is that there is one thing lacking in the sufferings of Jesus: *the love offering of Christ is to be presented in person through missionaries to the peoples for whom he died.* And Paul says he does this in his sufferings. '[I]n my flesh I am filling up what is lacking in Christ's afflictions'. Which means that Christ intends for the Great Commission to be a presentation to the nations of the sufferings of his cross through the sufferings of his people. That is the way it will be finished. If you sign up for the Great Commission, that is what you sign up for.

In the early 1990s, when I was working on the book *Let the Nations Be Glad!*[2] I hid away at Trinity Seminary in Deerfield, Illinois, on a writing leave. Then I got word that J. Oswald Sanders, the 89-year-old, veteran missions leader, was going to be in chapel. I wanted to hear him, so I sneaked into the back of chapel and listened to him. And this 89-year-old man stood up there, and I was just oozing with admiration and desire to be like that when I am 89. He told a story that embodies Colossians 1:24.

He said there was once an evangelist in India who trudged on foot to various villages preaching the gospel. He was a simple man with no education, who loved Jesus with all his heart, and was ready to lay down his life. He came to a village that did not have the gospel. It was late in the day and he was very tired. But he went into the village and lifted his voice and shared the gospel with those gathered in the square. They mocked him and drove him out of town. And he was so tired – with no emotional resources left – that he lay down under a tree, utterly discouraged. He went to sleep not knowing if he would ever wake up. They might come and kill him, for all he knew.

Suddenly, just after dusk, he was startled and woke up. The whole town seemed to be around him, looking at him. He thought he would probably die. One of the big men in the village said, 'We came out to see what kind of man you are, and when we saw your blistered feet we knew you were a holy man. We want you to tell us why you were willing to get blistered feet to come to talk to us.' So he preached the gospel, and, according to J. Oswald Sanders, the whole village believed. I think that's what Paul means by 'in my flesh I am filling up what is lacking in Christ's afflictions'.

I have one other small parenthesis about J. Oswald Sanders. At 89 years of age, he said, 'I've written a book a year since I was 70.' Eighteen books after 70! There are people in my church and all over America abandoning productive life at 65 and dying on the golf course, when they ought to be laying their lives down among the Muslims, like Raymond Lull did, who was a twelfth-century oriental scholar and missionary to Muslims. As he grew old he thought, 'What am I doing? I'm going to die here in Italy. Why not die in Algeria across the Mediterranean preaching the gospel?' And so, knowing what it would cost him to preach publicly, he boarded a boat at 80-something years of age and crossed the Mediterranean. He stayed underground for a while, encouraging the church, and then he decided it was as good a time as any. So he stood up and preached, and they killed him. What a way to go!

Why should we think that putting in our forty or fifty years on the job should mean that we should play games for the last fifteen years before we meet the King? This is biblically incomprehensible. We are strong at 65 and we are strong at 70. Don Carson, take note! You are entering a glorious chapter – at least eighteen more books! Or mission in some dangerous place.

My father, who died in 2007, was bursting with ministry in his late seventies and early eighties. I can remember twenty-five years before that, when my mother was killed, and he was almost killed, in a bus accident in Israel. I picked him up at the Atlanta airport along with my mother's body ten days after the accident. In the ambulance, all the way home from Atlanta to Greenville, South Carolina, he lay there with his back completely lacerated, and he kept saying, 'God must have a purpose for me; God must have a purpose for me!' He could not fathom that his wife of thirty-six years was gone and God had spared him. And indeed God did have a purpose for him. It was not long before his life exploded with new ministry, especially globally. He was working harder in his seventies for the nations than ever before. He prepared lessons from Easley, South Carolina, including some tapes, and they were used in sixty nations with about 10,000 people believing in Jesus every year, because God spared my dad and caused him not to believe in retirement.

The Prize Is Satisfying

How do you love like that? Where are you going to get this kind of courage and motivation? Are you feeling ready for this? Do you think you have it within you to be able to endure this?

Read Stephen Neill's *A History of Christian Missions*.[3] He describes what happened in Japan when Christianity came there in the 1500s. The emperor began to believe that the incursion of the Christian faith into their religious sphere was so threatening that they must end it. And he ended it with absolutely incredible brutality. It was over for the church in Japan. And I do not doubt that the hardness and difficulty of Japan today is largely owing to the massive (though short-term) triumph of the devil in the early 1600s.

Twenty-seven Jesuits, fifteen friars, and five secular clergy did manage to evade the order of banishment. It was not until April 1617 that the first martyrdoms of Europeans took place, a Jesuit and a Franciscan being beheaded at Omura at that time, and a Dominican and an Augustinian a little later in the same area. Every kind of cruelty was practised on the pitiable victims of the persecution. Crucifixion was the method usually employed in the case of Japanese Christians. On one occasion seventy Japanese at Yedo were crucified upside down at low water and were drowned as the tide came in.

I cried when I first read that, because I have a good enough imagination to picture the lapping water with your wife on one side and your 16-year-old on the other.

Are you ready? Do you think you have got that within you? You have not. No way does anybody have that kind of resourcefulness within. Where are we going to get it? This is where I want to close.

We are going to get it by believing the promises of God. Hebrews 10:32–34 is my favourite text about where we get the resources to live like this. '[R]ecall the former days when, after you were enlightened, you endured a hard struggle with sufferings, sometimes being publicly exposed to reproach and affliction, and sometimes being partners with those so treated'.

Now let me stop there and give you the situation. In the early days of the church, persecution arose. Some of them suffered outright and publicly, and others had compassion on them. You will see in the next verse that some of them were imprisoned and some of them went to visit them. So they were forced into a decision. Those who were in prison in those days probably depended on others for food and water and any kind of physical care that they would need.

But that meant that their friends and neighbours had to go public and identify with them. That is a risky business when someone has been put in jail because they are a Christian. So those who were still free went underground for a few hours (I am imagining this) and asked, 'What are we going to do?' And somebody said, 'Psalm 63:3 says that the steadfast love of the Lord is better than life. It's better than life. Let's go!' And if Martin Luther had been there he would have said, 'Let goods and kindred go, this mortal life also. The body they may kill, God's truth abideth still. His kingdom is for ever. Let's go!' And that's exactly what they did.

Here is the rest of the text (Heb. 10:34): '[Y]ou had compassion on those in prison, and you joyfully accepted the plundering of your property'. Now here is what happened. It does not take any imagination. I do not know all the details precisely, but here is what happened: they had compassion on the prisoners, which means they went to them. And their property – house, chariot, horses, mules, carpentry tools, chairs, whatever – was set on fire by a mob or maybe just ransacked and thrown to the streets by people with machetes. And when they looked over their shoulder to see what was happening back there, they *rejoiced*.

Now if you are not like these Christians – when somebody smashes your computer while you are trying to minister to them, or when you drive into the inner city to serve the poor, and they smash your windscreen, take your radio or slash your tyres – if you are not like these radical Christians in Hebrews 10:34, you are probably not going to be a very good candidate for martyrdom either. So the question is, 'How are we going to be like this?' I want to be like this. That is why I love this text!

I make no claim to be a perfect embodiment of this; but I want to be like this, so that when a stone comes sailing through my kitchen window – as it has done multiple times over the years – and smashes the glass and my wife and children hit the floor not knowing if it is a bullet or a grenade, I want to be able to say, 'Isn't this a great neighbourhood to live in? This is where the needs are. You see those five teenage kids that just rode by? They need Jesus. If I move out of here, who's going to tell them about Jesus?'

When your little boy gets pushed off his bicycle and they take it and run, I want to be able to take him by the neck while he is crying and say, 'Son, this is like being a missionary. It's like getting ready for the mission field! This is great!'

Now I haven't got to the main point of the text yet. How did they have the wherewithal to rejoice at the plundering of their property and the risking of their lives? Here's the answer: 'since you knew that you yourselves had a better possession and an abiding one.' Their love and their courage came from knowing they had a great reward beyond the grave. It was that real.

If you are a Christian, God is holding out to you indescribably wonderful promises. '"I will never leave you nor forsake you." So we can confidently say, "The Lord is my helper; I will not fear; what can man do to me?"' (Heb. 13:5–6). What can man do to you? Well, actually, man can kill you. But that is no final defeat, because we know what Romans 8:36–39 says:

> As it is written, 'For your sake we are being killed all the day long; we are regarded as sheep to be slaughtered.' No, in all these things we are more than conquerors through him who loved us. For I am sure that neither death nor life, nor angels nor rulers, nor things present nor things to come, nor powers, nor height nor depth, nor anything else in all creation, will be able to separate us from the love of God in Christ Jesus our Lord.'

Therefore, nothing ultimately can harm you.

Remember what Jesus said in Luke 21:16–18? '[S]ome of you they will put to death . . . But not a hair of your head will perish.' What does that mean: '[S]ome of you they will kill . . . But not a hair of your head will perish'? It is Romans 8:28. Everything, including death, works together for your good. When you die, you do not perish. To die is gain. Doing missions when death is gain is the greatest life in the world.[4]

Notes

1. Bible quotations in this chapter are from the English Standard Version. Italics are added by the author.
2. Grand Rapids, Mich.: Baker, 3rd ed., 2010.
3. London: Penguin, 2nd ed., 1986.
4. This chapter is an edited version of a message given at a special missions gathering at Wheaton College on 27 October 1996.